VO
FO
THEM

VOTE FOR THEM

David Edgar
and
Neil Grant

BBC BOOKS

Vote for Them was first shown on BBC 2.

Director	*James Ormerod*
Producer	*Carol Parks*
Executive Producer	*Michael Wearing*
Script Editors	*Estelle Daniel, Hilary Salmon*
Designer	*Nigel Jones*
Costume Designer	*Janice Rider*
Make-up Designer	*Gill Hughes*
Technical Adviser	*Bill Davidson*
Videotape Editor	*Steve Neilson*
Camera Supervisor	*David Doogood*
Sound	*Andy Redfern*
Lighting	*Barry Chatfield*

All photographs copyright BBC

Published by BBC Books,
a division of BBC Enterprises Limited,
Woodlands, 80 Wood Lane, London W12 0TT
First published 1989

© David Edgar and Neil Grant 1989

ISBN 0 563 21488 0

Set in 10 on 12pt Plantin by Ace Filmsetting Ltd, Frome
Printed and bound in Great Britain by
Redwood Burn Limited, Trowbridge, Wiltshire
Cover printed by Fletchers of Norwich

Introduction

I grew to political adulthood in the 1960s: a son of parents whose own
coming of age was celebrated in military uniform. Their accounts of World
War Two were ones prompted by a child's investigation of already faded
photograph albums, collections of monochrome and sepia which still seem
timeless. The young faces I now see were then of indeterminate age,
belonging only to the category of 'grown-ups'. They inhabited, in the 1950s,
a vanished and meaningless world, where people posed in rows under the
wings of aircraft or on the steps of anonymous mansions. I didn't
understand it, nor could a child be expected to. But that lack of
understanding later turned to tiredness and even to hostility. How often, I
wonder, can a generation have so comprehensively rejected the experience
of its parents as we did during the later 1960s – a period when any passing
memory of wartime service was, for me, associated with the daily horrors of
real and present conflicts? The Vietnam War and all it represented
generated an intolerance of memory, nullifying experiences and creating a
bar on any discussion or anecdote which sought to recover a positive
moment from World War Two.

Then, in November 1978, I read a *New Statesman* article by Edward
Thompson. Its subject was contemporary: a critique of official secrecy, but
suddenly it went much further:

'One is not permitted to speak of one's wartime reminiscences today, nor
is one under any impulse to do so. It is an area of general reticence: an
unmentionable subject among younger friends, and perhaps of mild ridicule
among those of radical opinions. All this is understood. And one
understands also why it is so.' I was alerted. He was talking about me and
to me: it was shockingly familiar. Continuing, he spoke of the way in which
the authoritarian Right had made an uncontested takeover of the moral
assets of the period. The dominant, received account was that of
Hollywood blockbusters, of paperbacks and 'television tedia' which
reinforced a unidimensional view of wartime. By contrast Thompson's
memory differed in many significant ways: 'I recall a resolute and
ingenious civilian army, increasingly hostile to the conventional military
virtues, which became – far more than any of my younger friends will begin
to credit – an anti-fascist and conspicuously anti-imperialist army. Its

members voted Labour in 1945: knowing why.'

I then began to recall fragments of conversation, of anecdotes from years before. I remembered stories of the wartime RAF, where rank and age relations were redefined: when a nineteen-year-old sergeant pilot might command a crew which was both older and often commissioned. Where slogans in support of the Soviet Union were the contemporary graffiti: 'Russia bleeds while Britain bullshits!' And this on a British airfield in wartime North Africa.

But, as Thompson had indicated, these were not the dominant memories, rather they were peripheral and incomplete: partial accounts which did not really belong in the familiar chronologies or accounts of grand strategy.

I was not without knowledge of the period, having read Angus Calder's excellent book *The People's War*, but had failed to appreciate that the young people who survived World War Two were now today's older generations: that their experiences lived with them, indeed had made them; that specific memories co-existed with a broader generational memory, subject frequently to modification and redefinition.

I began to wonder what a more integrated history might look like, and whether it was possible to redress the balance. Whether some 'hidden history' could be recovered and, perhaps, some amends made for a youthful dismissal of such formative experiences. Whether, indeed, I might be able to explore the period and discover something which was at variance with the received accounts current in the contemporary culture.

From all the half stories I had picked up over the years there was one which had long intrigued me, but suddenly it had an urgency about it. I knew only of the vaguest detail, and even suspected that it was apocryphal. The story was that there had once been a soldiers' parliament in Cairo which had, rather like the Putney Debates in the English Civil War, involved soldiers debating the purposes of the war and the nature of the post-war world. The version of the Cairo Parliament represented to me was akin to a soviet, romantic and mutinous in character. Beyond that I knew nothing. I resolved to discover more.

As with many 'discoveries' it transpires that they are that only for the person making them. To others it is all old hat.

In this case I quickly found, from published sources and in particular from a contemporary NCCL pamphlet, that the story of the events in Cairo was extensively recorded. What amazed me was that I had not known of it before, and that it was far more interesting than I could have imagined.

Recounting the essence of the story to friends of my generation, whose historical and political knowledge was otherwise extensive, the reaction was usually 'Tell us more, we've never heard of it.'

So it was, as a direct result of Thompson's journalistic prompting that, ten years ago, David Edgar and I began to discuss the phenomenon of 'forces' radicalism', our own lamentable lack of knowledge and the possibility of working on some kind of joint project to rectify that deficiency. David had already written a play, *The Dunkirk Spirit*, which referred to the way in which the memory of World War Two was exploited, and was keenly interested in documentary drama as a form. We also shared a broadly similar political orientation and perception.

We were both aware that in the year prior to the 1979 General Election the significance of 1945 was a recurrent, almost subliminal, theme in political discourse. An ascendant Conservatism was laying the foundations for an assault on the 'post-war settlement' and the broad 'Butskellite' consensus which had governed British politics since 1945. Our tentative project was concerned with recovering alternative accounts of developments prior to 1945. These, we hoped, might be shared with a larger audience, as one contribution to a contemporary re-evaluation of political culture in World War Two.

By 1981 David was able to propose an outline for a project to the BBC Drama Department at Pebble Mill, and subsequently secure a joint commission for us to research and write what we called *Vote for Them*. I was to take charge of the research, David the subsequent dramatisation. The central focus was to be the events surrounding the Cairo Parliament, based as far as possible on the testimony of surviving participants. We were looking, then, to secure an oral history as well as documentary base from which to tell the story.

Once we began to meet with those who were involved in the parliament a network became visible, even though people had not seen one another in more than thirty-five years. It was a delight to encounter so much enthusiasm and generosity, from people who had assumed that later generations cared little for their youthful exploits.

As documentary records, letters and diaries emerged we were provided with a graphic account of the events which had unfolded in Cairo between late 1943 and the spring of 1944. All this was given flesh and blood as we spoke with those who had actually organised things, had taken part in debates, written speeches and done the routine committee work. One former sergeant was even able to confide that he was the anonymous author of the cuttings from the *Egyptian Gazette* which I had acquired from other participants in the parliament. The Music for All Parliament, as it was properly called, was made possible by many earlier developments, and it is necessary to know something of these if the Cairo events are to be set properly in context and understood.

From 1941 onwards the British Army was subjected to an unprecedented educational programme, with the explicit intention of bolstering morale. Moreover, the central themes were concerned with social and political affairs. What had previously been anathema for the army – the open discussion of politics – was not only permitted, but actively encouraged. This, despite the existence of King's Regulations which apparently took a more censorial view of the soldier's political role, and the views of senior officers whose politics were of a more traditional nature.

All this paradoxical political debate was conducted under the auspices of the Army Bureau of Current Affairs or ABCA as it was universally known. ABCA issued fortnightly *Current Affairs* bulletins to army units, with the intention that they should be used as a basis for a discussion chaired by a unit officer. The bulletins covered a wide range of topical themes, but often focused on the nature of the post-war world and the problems which would have to be faced. One of the principal intentions of ABCA was to give the 'citizens in uniform' the opportunity to express themselves. Debate was to be approved and institutionalised.

A host of other publications and schemes accompanied, or were spawned by, the ABCA initiative, within the army, navy and air force. Educational activity, and in particular informed discussion, was pursued as vital to good morale. ABCA's own publicity even drew on a republican tradition, quoting Cromwell's dictum, 'The citizen soldier must know what he is fighting for, and love what he knows.'

In the Cairo of September 1943, with the locus of action no longer in the neighbouring desert but across the sea in Italy, the frenetic times were over. Large numbers of people, based in and around Cairo, had more free time than they had experienced for years. The service clubs provided opportunities for meeting and discussing, and routine educational work continued in army units and on airfields. But inertia and boredom were ever-present threats, as weeks turned into months, with little prospect of movement. Inevitably, those service people with a serious interest in politics came together, to discuss and also to participate in forms of political action which were available to them. For some this was to be the enthusiastic pursuit of novel forms of political expression and the 'mock parliament' was just such a form.

The mock parliament was a familiar debating vehicle in the 1930s, with regular 'parliaments' at Twickenham, Hampstead and Birmingham's Winson Green, to name but three. In essence it was a debating forum, organised on parliamentary lines and according to parliamentary procedure. The model was endorsed as appropriate for civic education by prominent educationalists, and many people in the forces would certainly have taken part in something similar during their schooldays. There were also precedents for forces' parliaments, with one on Gibraltar earlier in the war.

The venue for the 'parliament' in Cairo was a large services' centre, Music for All, catering for all ranks and a wide range of interests. Housed in what had formerly been a cinema, Music for All had already become a base for the poets of the Salamander Society. It also served as a meeting place for a discussion group, 'Thinking Aloud', and it was from the discussion group that the decision to hold a parliament emerged. The Music for All Parliament was to meet only five times, once a month from December 1943 to April 1944. The sessions lasted two hours and were open to all who paid the admission fee, irrespective of rank or service. As it developed it attracted hundreds of interested participants, eventually packing a hall which could accommodate 750. It also prompted a number of others on RAF stations near Cairo. It was therefore not alone in the Middle East, though it was the only one to be reported around the world and subsequently discussed in the House of Commons!

The story which we tell in *Vote for Them* is of this parliament and other events which some of its participants were involved in. All the situations described are based on real incidents recounted to us, while the sequence of parliaments is broadly that of the real ones. The meetings actually took place, and many of the speeches are based on notes and documents produced at the time. There has, of course, also been much invention which we hope is faithful to the spirit of the time.

We do, however, make one important qualification. This is that all the characters have been fictionalised, with many conflated from two or more real people. They have therefore no living counterparts. We have been fortunate to talk with many of the leading figures in the parliament, and while they may recognise features and attributes of particular friends or acquaintances they will search in vain for the identity of others.

It is our hope that, in *Vote for Them*, we have a story which is recognisable to those who were there and prompts further enquiry by those who weren't. Above all, we hope that the many people who have given their time and shared memories with us will feel that the story we tell is theirs too.

Neil Grant
January 1989

Characters

THE SPEAKER
Lieutenant David Rubin, UDF   *Nicholas Jones*

THE GOVERNMENT
Aircraftsman Gerry ('Nobby') Clarke   *Simon Adams*
Sergeant Alistair McRae, RASC   *Billy Hartman*
Warrant Officer Steve Wilson, RAOC   *Jeff Rawle*
Sergeant Jack Simpson, REME   *Andrew Paul*
Leading Aircraftsman Neville Atterley   *John Wheatley*
Signalman Alfred Jacobs   *David Cardy*

THE OPPOSITION
Major John Trapnell, AEC   *David Quilter*
Captain Cecil Carrington, RASC   *Nicholas Day*
Corporal Hugh Leslie, RAPC   *Christopher Baines*
Corporal Douglas Richardson   *Patrick Pearson*
Captain Graham Castle, AEC   *Christopher Scoular*
Flight Sergeant Geoffrey Carter   *Robin Davies*
Flight Lieutenant Frank Trelawney   *Nicholas Frankau*

THE BRASS
The Brigadier   *James Grout*
Colonel Raymond Pugh, AEC   *John Rowe*
The General   *Richard Bebb*
Signals Colonel   *Martin Cochrane*
Another Colonel   *Robert Gary*

BACKBENCHERS
Angry Wren   *Kathryn Hurlbutt*
Geordie ATS   *Mary Nuttall*
Lancastrian Sergeant   *James Mansfield*
Padre   *James Snell*
American Journalist   *Hu Pryce*

MUSIC FOR ALL
The Director   *Kathleen Bidmead*
Dr Brent Garfield   *Peter Dennis*
Assistant (Bookstall)   *Eileen Kenning*
Admissions Clerks   *Louise Papillon, Ruth Hellier*

AS YOU LIKE IT
The Producer   *Terry Molloy*
Rosalind   *Jane Gurnett*
Amiens   *Malcolm McKee*
Duke Senior   *Pat Connell*

RAF HELIOPOLIS
Aircraftsman Bill Beatty   *Peter Ll. Williams*
Leading Aircraftsman (Truck)   *Barry Lowen*
Flight Sergeant   *Karl Jenkinson*
June   *Claire Toeman*

OTHERS
Charlotte Gluck   *Tusse Silberg*
Staff Sergeant Bill Ballantine, RASC   *Steve McFadden*
Ioannis   *Alkis Kritikos*
Greeks   *Dimitri Andreas, Ned Vukovic*
South Africans   *Luke Brannigan, Erik Collinson, Robert Frank*
Egyptian Policeman   *Tano Rea*
Captain (Embarkation Unit)   *Phillip Manikum*
First Sergeant (Embarkation Unit)   *Russell Glead*
GHQ Corporal   *Roy Leighton*
RAF Corporal (Forces Forum)   *Steven Brough*

THE PRESENT DAY
Alistair McRae   *Joseph Brady*
Steve Wilson   *Hugh Dickson*
Gerry Clarke   *Eric Mason*

Episode One

Footage: 1943 Army Film Unit.

A real film, available from the Imperial War Museum. The first shots are of a history book and The Modern Soldier, *with an accompanying commentary. Then there is footage of the Eighth Army in the desert.*

COMMENTARY. Three hundred years ago an Englishman, Oliver Cromwell, said these words: 'The citizen soldier must know what he is fighting for, and love what he knows.' In that spirit Cromwell created a New Army, of the finest fighting men England had to that day known. We've done it again. Britain has made another new army. These men are tough. The experience of three years of war has gone into their training and into their weapons. And each man as he goes into battle carries not only his arms and his technical military skill. Like the old Ironsides he takes something more – a weapon of the mind.

Exterior. The Egyptian Desert, September 1943. Day.

Dust. A man in khaki shorts and a shirt is sitting by the roadside. He has a large haversack. A truck appears in the distance. It is full of British airmen, who have just arrived in Egypt. It approaches the man. He is a British Army NCO – Sergeant McRae. He stands, and hardly needs to raise his thumb before the truck stops. The fresh-faced young airmen watch as McRae shouts to the driver, who sits in his cab with the Leading Aircraftsman in charge of the unit.

MCRAE. Eh, pal, is this by any chance the 27B for Cairo?

DRIVER. Heliopolis. Hop in.

MCRAE. Well, thank you ever so.

   McRae hops into the back of the truck. The only space is near the cab at the front. As he arrives there, he calls out:

MCRAE. Hold *very* tight please, now. Ting ting.

   McRae taps the top of the cab with each 'ting'. In the cab, the driver confides in the LAC, as he puts the truck in gear and drives off:

DRIVER. Base wallahs. GHQ. Since Alamein, they think the war's a bleeding holiday.

Exterior. Desert. Day.

In the back of the truck. McRae sitting near two young airmen, Clarke and Beatty, who, we'll discover, are from Birmingham. McRae looks at the young men with their white faces and knees.

MCRAE. So. Just off the boat then, are you?

CLARKE. Ar.

   McRae smiles.

MCRAE. So what d'you think?

   Beatty and Clarke don't understand.

BEATTY. What of, Sarge?

MCRAE. (*With a wave.*) Sunny Egypt. First impressions. The very first thing that you thought.

Beatty and Clarke look at each other. A raised eyebrow, a shrug.

BEATTY. It's effing hot.

McRae smiles.

MCRAE. It is indeed.

He reaches into his haversack and takes out a newspaper. He opens it, affects to read. Then:

I'm sorry. Either of you fellows want a paper?

Clarke and Beatty think that McRae wants to give them his only paper.

Hot off the presses too.

He takes two other copies of the same paper from his haversack, and hands them over. Clarke and Beatty look at the papers. The title is STRAIGHT TALK, subtitled 'Middle East Anti-Fascist News'. The headline reads: 'British workers and soldiers demand: ALL FOR THE ANGLO-SOVIET ALLIANCE.' A sub-headline reads: 'Salute to the Red Army.' Clarke and Beatty look at each other again, and at McRae.

CLARKE. Uh, what –

MCRAE. Never you mind.

Before Clarke can respond, another airman draws McRae's attention to a clearly unwell airman beside him. McRae taps the back window of the cab and gestures to the LAC to stop. In the cab, the LAC tells the driver:

LAC. I think we better stop.

As the driver pulls in to the side of the road, Beatty, grinning:

BEATTY. Eh. 'Ere we go.

The truck stops. The unwell airman jumps down off the back of the truck, as the LAC gets down from the cab. Clarke is still looking with puzzled interest at the paper and McRae.

Exterior. Desert. Day.

McRae is sitting on the sand, near the truck, rolling a cigarette. In the distance are a couple of Egyptian peasants. Clarke comes up to McRae. He has a lit cigarette, and matches.

CLARKE. Do you want a light, Sarge?

MCRAE. Well, that is very kind.

Clarke lights McRae's cigarette. Then he looks out across the desert. McRae clocks this and looks up at him.

A touch more space than Longbridge.

CLARKE. (*Slight smile, embarrassed.*) Quinton.

MCRAE. Have you read T. E. Lawrence? Lawrence of Arabia?

CLARKE. No.

MCRAE. *The Seven Pillars of Wisdom.* Worth a try.

Clarke tries to come up with the correct response. Feeling he's failed, he turns to go.

So what's your racket? Rigger?

CLARKE. Fitter.

MCRAE. Sound browned off.

CLARKE. Well, my brother's aircrew. Italy.

MCRAE. So you fancy being in the fighting, then?

CLARKE. Well, not exactly in –

Beatty approaches.

BEATTY. Bloody hell, Nob, what's all this? You got the sun, the sea, no blackout, lots of wogs to run about for you and all them luscious gyppo bints . . . And you want to get your balls blown off in Itiland?

The LAC, a little distant:

LAC. Right, you lot! Back aboard!

MCRAE. (*To Beatty.*) Well, you certainly been picking up the lingo.

Slight pause.

Well, you heard the LAC.

BEATTY. Yes, Sarge.

Beatty goes off towards the truck. Clarke stays with McRae a moment, looking out towards the desert.

MCRAE. You see, I thought you'd say the poverty.

CLARKE. Beg pardon?

MCRAE. First impressions. Thought you'd say, the beggars and the starving in the streets. What sixty-seven years of British occupation does to you.

Slight pause. He turns to go back towards the truck. As he goes:

'Cos that's what first struck me.

Clarke hurries to catch him up, glancing at the newspaper in his hand.

CLARKE. So, Sarge . . . are you . . . There was this bloke in Lancashire, or Cheshire, somewhere, won a seat against the Government? The Common – something?

They're at the truck. As McRae grasps the rail to heave himself in, to Clarke:

MCRAE. Wealth. No, that's not us.

Exterior. Desert. Day.

McRae sitting with Beatty and Clarke in the truck as it bounces along.

MCRAE. So how's tricks back in Blighty?

CLARKE. Pretty bad.

Slight pause.

BEATTY. Well for some. My sister thinks it's grand. She earns more than my Dad now, at the Austin.

MCRAE. So you were both in motors?

CLARKE. Bill was.

Slight pause.

Me, I'd never touched a motor till I got called up. Didn't know I'd got the touch, like.

BEATTY. Well, you hadn't.

MCRAE. Ah, well, as they say . . .

CLARKE. In fact, as time goes by, you get to know how bloody much you don't. If you, like follow me.

McRae looks at Clarke.

MCRAE. Oh, aye. Indeed.

Exterior. Heliopolis RAF camp: outside main gate. Day.

The truck approaches the barrier at the main gate of Heliopolis RAF camp. The truck stops, the driver waves a chitty, the barrier is raised.

Exterior. Heliopolis RAF camp: inside main gate. Day.

The truck has come through the main gate and comes to a stop. McRae is scribbling a number on a scrap of paper. A couple of RAF NCOs are standing near the gate, watching and smoking. The LAC hops out of the cab to speak to McRae.

LAC. OK, Sarge?

MCRAE. Champion. (*As he stands, he slips the note to Clarke.*) My name's McRae. My number. Ring me there, OK? (*Less privately, as he hoists his haversack and hops off the truck.*) And p'raps we'll meet up when your knees get brown.

CLARKE. Yuh, right.

McRae walks over to the NCOs.

MCRAE. (*Grandly.*) Now, gents, I am expected for a chota with the Brig at half past five . . .

And we hear the voice of the present-day McRae as we mix into:

Interior. Heliopolis RAF camp: hangar. Morning.

A huge, more or less empty aircraft hangar. Clarke and Beatty stand in the doorway, framed by the fierce light of the morning sun. They look at each other and walk into the hangar. We hear the older McRae:

MCRAE. (*Voice over.*) Now you see, for those of us in Cairo, we were still busy with administration, maintenance, repair work and the like, but basically by now the actual war had moved on into Italy. And the Army's educational endeavours, ABCA training and the like, had excited interest in discussion of current affairs. And in Cairo you had service clubs and places where you could pursue your interests in your leisure hours, whether that was music, drama, or political discussion. And, in our case, yes, a certain element of mischief and intrigue.

And by now we have mixed into:

Exterior. Street. Early evening.

Outside 'Music for All', a services club in Cairo. A sign:

'Music for All
Officers, NCOs, and men of the Allied forces.
Concerts, Talks, Reading Rooms, Bridge, Baths, Restaurant, Tea Garden etc.'

A jeep arrives, driven by Beatty. Clarke, closing his services guide, which includes his map, gets out of the jeep. Beatty drives off.

Interior. Music for All: lobby. Early evening.

Music for All used to be a cinema, and some of its fixtures and decorations betray its past, though it is by no means seedy, and in some of its aspects even 'palm court'. In the lobby there is – permanently – an admissions booth staffed by a woman civilian, and a bookstall, staffed by an assistant. At the moment, there is also a small party waiting for the arrival of important personages. The party consists of the Director of Music for All and the (American) Literary Director, Dr Brent Garfield. Suddenly, there is activity, as the officers enter: the Brigadier commanding 17 Area, British Troops in Egypt, Colonel Raymond Pugh, Education Officer-in-Chief, Middle East Forces, and Major John Trapnell, also of the Army Education Corps.

DIRECTOR. Brigadier, welcome to Music for All.

BRIGADIER. My pleasure, Ma'am.

DIRECTOR. Now, do you know Dr Garfield, of the American University?

As she introduces Garfield, we move out of earshot, to the point of view of Nobby Clarke, who is at the bookstall, with a book in his hand. He watches the two groups introduced, and then the Director gently ushering them towards the main part of the building. He puts the book back. The Assistant appears.

ASSISTANT. Um – was there anything that I could help you with?

Clarke looks at a note in his hand.

CLARKE. Yes, I'm looking for a book by – T. E. Lawrence.

ASSISTANT. *Seven Pillars?* You might find it in the library . . .

CLARKE. I see.

Interior. Music for All: music room. Early evening.

The Brigadier, the Director, Pugh, Trapnell, Garfield and the others stand at the back of a gramophone concert: a reasonably large crowd of service people, sitting in armchairs listening to baroque music on gramophone records. As in all Music for All crowds, there should be a wide variety of uniforms, and some Indians and black Americans as well as the usual sprinklings of New Zealanders, Australians, Canadians, South Africans and Greeks along with the British. A moment or two, then:

BRIGADIER. Is this – this is Mozart?

DIRECTOR. Uh, Handel, I think, actually.

Interior. Music for All: lobby. Early evening.

Clarke wandering towards the admissions booth as Sergeant Jack Simpson enters the lobby from the street. He goes to the admissions booth, and shows his season ticket.

SIMPSON. Hallo there, gorgeous.

The Clerk nods, acknowledging, as Simpson walks on. Clarke comes up to the booth.

CLARKE. Excuse me . . . I'm looking for a Sergeant, Alistair McRae.

ADMISSIONS CLERK. Oh, he'll be in political discussion. In the Garden Room.

Clarke looks blank.

Just follow him . . .

Clarke sets off after Simpson.

Interior. Music for All: corridor. Early evening.

Outside the Garden Room. Clarke catches up with Simpson.

CLARKE. Uh – is this where the discussion, Sarge . . . ?

Leading Airman Neville Atterley is coming out of the room.

SIMPSON. It is, old lad. (*To Atterley.*) Hey, Neville, where are you skiving off to?

ATTERLEY. Special duties, comrade.

Simpson affects a 'nudge, nudge' reaction as Atterley hurries off down the corridor. Then, opening the door to let Clarke in:

SIMPSON. I wouldn't bother with the 'Sarge'.

Interior. Music for All: corridor. Early evening.

The Brigadier, the Director, Pugh, Trapnell, Garfield and the others proceeding along the corridor. Atterley appears from the other end.

DIRECTOR. The building housed a cinema, originally. Bit of a flea pit, if the truth be told.

Atterley, having sized up the situation, turns smartly and goes back whence he came. The Director's party has reached its next port of call, the Library, and Garfield opens the door, with a little 'shh' gesture, as he does so.

Interior. Music for All: corridor. Early evening.

Atterley hurries back to the Garden Room, scribbling a note on a piece of paper as he goes, and enters.

Interior. Music for All: Garden Room. Early evening.

The discussion group is not very large: even with Simpson and Clarke, there are a number of empty seats. The speaker is Warrant Officer Steve Wilson, in his late twenties; the chair is McRae. On an easel is a chart of the British political system: the political parties leading into the House of Commons, connected with the Lords and the Crown above, with sub-branches for Law Lords, Committees, Privy Council and the other branches of state, and local government below. In fact, however, Wilson is talking about something quite different.

WILSON. And indeed it's worth noting –

He stops as Atterley enters. Seeing it's Atterley, Wilson carries on, as Atterley scribbles a note.

– that Egypt isn't now and never has been an actual colony. It is ruled by a puppet leader – King Farouk – in the interests, and under the protection, of the imperialistic power.

Atterley hands the note to McRae, who slides it over to Wilson, as:

Which is not to say that the indigenous ruling class is not to blame for the disparities of wealth which are obvious to everyone. Indeed, the custom of landowners demanding half the produce of the land they rent –

Wilson looks at the note, nods almost imperceptibly to Atterley, who goes out.

– is about as pure an example of the theory of surplus value as you could find.

A keen, but embarrassed, group member puts his hand up.

KEEN MEMBER. I'm sorry, Mr Chairman, could the speaker just run through the surplus value business once again . . . ?

Groans.

WILSON. All right.

More groans.

Now, there's this man who owns a biscuit factory –

Interior. Music for All: Library. Early evening.

The Brigadier, the Director, Pugh, Trapnell, Garfield and the others are standing at the back of the Library, where a read-through of As You Like It *is going on. Most of the actors are in uniform of one kind or another. They're on Act Two, Scene Four. The Producer of the play keeps glancing at his watch. Rosalind is a Jewish ATS girl.*

ROSALIND. I prithee, shepherd, if that love or gold
Can in this desert place buy entertainment,
Bring us where we may rest ourselves and feed.

Atterley hurries in, past the Director's party. The Producer looks at him and taps his watch.

ATTERLEY. I'm sorry.

Garfield, the Director and Trapnell smile. Garfield gestures the party out.

ROSALIND. Here's a young maid with travel much oppress'd,
And faints for succour.

Interior. Music for All: corridor. Early evening.

The Brigadier, the Director, Pugh, Trapnell, Garfield and the others proceeding down the corridor.

DIRECTOR. They do have a problem, with the plays, and people being posted during the rehearsals.

GARFIELD. Yuh, they did *Major Barbara* here last year, and by the time they got it on, they were on to their fourth Undershaft.

Trapnell and Pugh laugh.

BRIGADIER. I'm sorry, Major who?

Luckily, they have arrived at the door to the Garden Room.

DIRECTOR. Now this is Dr Garfield's territory.

She opens the door slowly, so as not to make a noise.

Interior. Music for All: Garden Room. Early evening.

From the point of view of the entering group – the Brigadier, the Director, Pugh, Trapnell, Garfield and the others – we see Wilson lecturing on the structure of the British political system, tapping at the easel, eagerly listened to by, among others, McRae, Simpson and Clarke.

WILSON. – to form a government. Thus the ordinary citizen can influence the policy of his country at several stages. First, he –or she – can join a party, and participate in its discussions on this policy or that. He can write to the papers, and join a campaign for anything from Justice for India to Pensions for Spinsters –

A little laugh. This time it is Pugh who, glancing at his watch, gestures to the rest of the party to go, which they do.

– and he can play his humble but vitally important part in turning out the Government at the next election. And it will be noted that this system is the opposite to that which operates in a dictatorship like . . .

The visiting party have gone. Wilson is quickly back into the real subject.

. . . Germany, but the point is that if Bath Oliver is going to make a surplus, then his workers won't be able to buy back the biscuits that they make for him, and he'll overproduce, and create an economic crisis. And, as Karl Marx puts it in the pamphlet 'Wages Price and Profit', that will inevitably lead –

Interior. Music for All: corridor. Early evening.

The Brigadier, the Director, Pugh, Trapnell, Garfield and the others walking back down the corridor.

BRIGADIER. So, putting ABCA out of business, Dr Garfield?

GARFIELD. Well, we have talks on a wide variety of topics. Often the most popular are hobbies: mountaineering, stamp-collecting, that kind of thing.

BRIGADIER. Ah. Prefer philately to politics?

GARFIELD. Well, no, I wouldn't say –

DIRECTOR. Or, sometimes, even, Paganini.

They are approaching the lobby.

BRIGADIER. Of course, the reason ABCA gets a full house, Dr Garfield, is not so much a burning urge to understand the British constitution, but because it's in work time, and it's compulsory.

We catch sight of Pugh glancing at Trapnell: they neither of them agree with this perspective of the Brigadier. At the entrance to the lobby, the Brigadier, realising he may have come on a little strong, and is now leaving, turns to the Director and Garfield.

But nonetheless – a splendid show.

The Director smiles and gestures the Brigadier and his party towards the entrance. They move.

Interior. Music for All: lobby. Early evening.

The music we heard at the beginning of this sequence swells as the Brigadier, the Director, Pugh, Trapnell, Garfield and the others, enter; the Brigadier's RSM comes to attention, the Brigadier shakes the Director's hand, and the Brass leave, followed by the Sergeant. The music climaxes. The guests are gone. The Director imitates a siren.

GARFIELD. Uh – what?

DIRECTOR. All clear.

Interior. Music for All: Garden Room. Early evening.

The meeting has finished. Wilson and Simpson are arguing in a corner. McRae is packing up papers. Clarke approaches.

CLARKE. Uh – Sarge.

McRae looks up to Clarke: ranks aren't used in Music for All.

MCRAE. Well, if it's no the Brummie. And how are tricks with you?

CLARKE. I'm fine. I rang your number. They said you were here most evenings.

MCRAE. And you found your way all right?

Clarke has his services' guide in his top pocket, turned to the map. He pats it.

CLARKE. I got dropped off.

McRae walks out of the room, expecting Clarke to follow, which he does.

Interior. Music for All: corridor. Early evening.

Clarke hurries out after McRae.

CLARKE. Grand place.

MCRAE. Aye, well. The Director's married to the Chief of Police.

Clarke looks at McRae.

She's, you know, one of those grand English ladies you find serving soup out to the needy on four continents. Just here, it's no soup but Shaw and Shostakovich.

CLARKE. I – I tried to get that book you said. The Seven Pillars thing.

Interior. Music for All: lobby. Early evening.

They come into the lobby. At the admissions booth, we are aware of someone asking for someone else, in a mixture of English and Greek.

MCRAE. Well, no, they wouldna have that here. In fact, it might be tricky to locate . . . But as it happens, did you say 'dropped off'?

Clarke is thrown by McRae's non sequitur.

CLARKE. That's right.

Slight pause.

MCRAE. Off what?

CLARKE. A jeep.

MCRAE. Whose jeep?

CLARKE. Our Flight. He's off sick and we got it for the week.

Slight pause.

Uh – as it happens, what?

MCRAE. (*A great deal more solicitous.*) Well, as it happens there's a bookshop, as it happens run by a close friend of mine, who as it happens you should meet.

CLARKE. Where is it?

MCRAE. It's not too far. But, in fact, I wouldn't go there totally directly.

CLARKE. No?

The Greek soldier spots McRae and comes over. He stands, politely, waiting for the conversation to end.

MCRAE. No, what I'd do, if I was for the sake of argument to happen to go there tomorrow, what I'd do, is I'd get myself dropped off at, say, the metro terminus, and then I'd mosey up Sharia Fouad el Awal, past the Ezbekieh Gardens to the opera, turn right down Sharia Kasr el Nil past Barclays to Mustafa Mamel roundabout, it's to your right, can't miss it.

McRae has spotted the Greek.

Say, half past two tomorrow? See you then.

He pats Clarke's arm and goes to the soldier. Clarke wanders back to the bookstall.

Well, hallo, Ioannis, what can I do for you?

Ioannis takes a rolled-up stencil from his pocket and presses it on McRae as he leads him out of Clarke's earshot.

IOANNIS. Now, Alistair, vital that you print the leaflet very pronto, else we do not have the soldiers from the camp . . .

Exterior. Cairo roundabout. Afternoon.

Clarke in Mustafa Mamel Square. He looks at the imposing statue at the centre. He spots the Rond Point bookshop and goes towards it.

Interior. Bookshop: main area. Afternoon.

The Rond Point bookshop is long and thin, with books laid out on large, coffin-like tables as well as on shelves. At the back there is a doorway leading to stairs down to a basement. The bookshop is run by Charlotte Gluck, an Egyptian woman of French–Jewish origin, who is setting out stock, helped by an assistant. Elsewhere, McRae has found The Seven Pillars of Wisdom *and hands it to Clarke.*

MCRAE. There you go, Nobby.

Clarke feels in his pocket for money.

CLARKE. Um . . .

McRae looks to Charlotte.

MCRAE. Look, why not borrow it for now? You want to keep it, pop back in and settle then. Is it OK to loan out *Seven Pillars*, Charley?

CHARLOTTE. The fine is three piastres and a public flogging. Does he want a cup of tea?

CLARKE. Who, me? Oh, thank you very much.

CHARLOTTE. (*In French.*) It's the normal Penguins at the back, and the specials at the front, Emile.

Charlotte leads Clarke and McRae to the exit to the basement.

Interior. Bookshop: basement. Early evening.

In the basement is a table, some chairs, piles of books and cartons, marked with countries of origin. Also a gas ring on which a kettle is gently simmering, near a teapot and mugs. At the table sit Wilson and Atterley, the former smoking a pipe and writing, the other reading. McRae, Clarke and Charlotte come down the stairs and enter the room.

MCRAE. Steve Wilson, Neville Atterley. Meet –

CLARKE. Well, it's actually Gerry. But the surname being 'Clarke' –

MCRAE. Meet Nobby.

WILSON. Hallo, there.

ATTERLEY. Do sit down.

Clarke sits.

MCRAE. Steve and Neville are the backbone of *Straight Talk*.

CLARKE. Oh, right.

Charlotte is pouring hot water into the teapot. A slight look over, at McRae. Wilson and Atterley glance at each other.

In fact, when my sis's bloke was square-bashing, they had a – well, he said, a blood-red bolshie. And there was this real bastard of a Sergeant, who had 'em on guard duty at all hours. And he, this bolshie character, says look, we got to find a way to protest which won't get us on a charge. So what he does is this. Each day, there's something left undone. So, on Monday, no one's done their gaiters. Tuesday, no one's polished up their buckles. Wednesday, when he says left turn, they all go right.

Slight pause. Charlotte is putting milk and sugar in two cups as she waits for the tea to mash. Clarke is aware that his anecdote is not going quite as well as usual.

Soon changed his tune.

There's usually a laugh at this point.

He used to say, this chap, apparently, he used to tell 'em: a bayonet's a length of steel with a worker at both ends.

WILSON. Oh, well, I'd imagine, that was in the early days. A different kind of war, since then.

CLARKE. How's that?

WILSON. Now the Soviet Union's involved.

Slight pause.

MCRAE. You see, Nob, since they took in Russia, it's no longer just an imperialist war, just carving up commercial markets in the interest of the ruling classes of both sides. Now it's a war of liberation from the yoke of fascist tyranny, in which the great democracies are on the same side as the world's first workers' state.

Slight pause.

WILSON. Which is why we're behind the war effort one hundred per cent.

MCRAE. In fact, sometimes, more so than the brass.

WILSON. A lot more.

ATTERLEY. Say two hundred then.

Charlotte puts Clarke's and McRae's teas on the table, pointedly.

CHARLOTTE. Your tea then, Mr Nobby Clarke.

CLARKE. Thank you.

Wilson stands. Charlotte sits.

WILSON. Alistair.

McRae realises that Wilson wants a private word. They move away from the others. Pause. Clarke smiles at Charlotte.

CHARLOTTE. So how did you meet Alistair?

CLARKE. Oh, in the desert, actually. Hitching a lift.

ATTERLEY. Well, you don't say.

Apart from the others, Wilson and McRae speak with lowered voices.

WILSON. So, Alistair, what is he?

MCRAE. What he looks like.

WILSON. And you're sure that he's all right?

MCRAE. What, you mean, not in the pay of the Gestapo?

WILSON. Or the SIB.

MCRAE. Yes, of course I'm sure. He's first rate. And he has apparently boundless access to vehicular impedimenta.

Slight pause.

Such as we have some need of in 'Operation Cardinal'.

There is a slight pause before Wilson shrugs and, with McRae, walks back to the table.

WILSON. (*Arriving.*) Well, um, Nobby, and how are you liking Cairo?

CLARKE. Oh, it's fine, um. Grand.

Pause.

As they say, all human life is here.

WILSON. Indeed.

He sits, followed by McRae.

It is. Which is actually of interest to us, us on *Straight Talk*, on account of, well, a good proportion of that human life consisting of the exiled armies of the Balkan countries.

CLARKE. Uh, beg pardon?

WILSON. Look, simply – Nobby, there is something you could do for us. We have a need for cloth.

CLARKE. For cloth.

CHARLOTTE. That's right. Material.

MCRAE. Just anything that you can scrounge.

WILSON. Ribbons. Towelling.

CHARLOTTE. Just anything that can be cut or sewn.

MCRAE. Just as much as you can manage to get hold of.

WILSON. By tomorrow night.

CLARKE. What for?

Pause. Atterley reaches over to where Clarke's copy of the Lawrence lies beside him on the table, he pulls it over to him, finds a passage, and reads:

ATTERLEY. 'The morning freshness of the world-to-be intoxicated us. We were wrought up with ideas vaporous and inexpressible, but to be fought for. Yet when we achieved, and the new world dawned, the old men came out again, and took our victory to remake in the likeness of the former world they knew. Youth could win, but it had not learned to keep; and was pitiably weak against the new age. We stammered that we had been working for a new heaven and a new earth, and they thanked us kindly and made their peace.'

He turns the book over and pushes it, still open, back over the table to Clarke. Everyone looks at him.

CLARKE. Uh . . . any preference to colour?

Wilson looks at Clarke.

Interior. Heliopolis RAF camp: hangar. Day.

Clarke is in the hangar. No one else is there. He goes into a little recess. No one is there either. Clarke is about to go back out when he notices a bit of red curtaining on a small window. He looks round, goes and takes the curtaining down. In a basket in the corner are all kinds of bits of rag: Clarke goes through and gets out three or four pieces of various shades of red. Then he sees over the back of the chair a bright red bandana. He picks it up and looks at it. There is a voice from behind. It's Beatty.

BEATTY. (*Out of vision.*) Hey, naughty, naughty, Nobby.

Clarke turns, guilty.

CLARKE. Uh – Uh, I . . .

Beatty takes a letter from his pocket and gives it to Clarke.

BEATTY. This came for you.

CLARKE. Oh, thanks.

Clarke takes the letter. He's about to open it, when his antennae pick up something from Beatty.

Did you hear anything?

BEATTY. Yuh. Apparently my sis has got herself a Yank.

Clarke smiles.

And my dad's been and gone and got his left hand caught up in his lathe, and it's gone septic.

Clarke looks up, concerned. Beatty grins.

And the bugger is, the sod's left-handed.

Slight pause.

Effing profiteers.

Beatty smiles, a little grimly, and turns to go. Then Clarke remembers.

CLARKE. Um – Um, Bill . . .

BEATTY. Yuh, what?

CLARKE. This afternoon. Uh, I wonder if you'd see your way –

Suddenly, a Flight Sergeant runs in.

BEATTY. Now, Nob –

FLIGHT SERGEANT. Ah. Here you are.

CLARKE. Hey, Flight –

The Flight Sergeant pulls open drawers, looking for files.

FLIGHT SERGEANT. Now, gentlemen. On the wire from Alex. Three Kitties and a Tommo, in all kinds of shit, needed back in Sicily by yesterday.

He takes his bandana from Clarke, and twirls it round his neck.

FLIGHT SERGEANT. And, thank you, Airman. Yes. I'm much improved.

Interior. Lobby. Day.

The lobby of a block of flats, army offices. By the stairs stands Staff Sergeant Ballantine, with a pile of bicycles in front of him.

CLARKE. (*Out of vision, sharply.*) Public Relations? Sergeant McRae?

Clarke stands in the doorway to the lobby, framed in the harsh light from the street. He carries his kitbag, now overstuffed with booty, held in front of him. He spots Ballantine's stripes. Mollified:

Staff Sergeant?

BALLANTINE. Sure, mate. Show you.

He picks up two of the bicycles.

Look, mate, any chance of giving us a hand?

CLARKE. (*With his kitbag.*) Erm . . .

Slight pause. He puts down the kitbag.

Yuh. Sure.

Interior. GHQ Public Relations: corridor. Day.

Ballantine and Clarke are seen carrying two bicycles each along a corridor from the top of the stairs.

Interior. GHQ Public Relations: office. Day.

The office has a duplicator, three desks and a noticeboard. At first, we see a leaflet coming through the duplicator. It's in Greek script, scratched on to the stencil – in fact, the stencil we saw Ioannis handing McRae in Music for All. McRae is working the duplicator.

BALLANTINE. Hey, Alistair. A friend.

McRae looks up, to see Ballantine, carrying two bicycles, in the corridor. Clarke appears with another two bikes. Two men framed in the doorway of the office.

MCRAE. Oh, hi there, Nobby.

Clarke puts his bikes down.

Eh, I trust those boneshakers aren't cluttering up our office.

BALLANTINE. Boneshakers nothing, mate. Five real racers, compliments the RAF. And they're going in the cuttings room. And so – hands off.

Ballantine goes off down the corridor. Clarke comes into the room.

MCRAE. Now, Nobby, did you get the stuff?

CLARKE. Oh, ar. I got the stuff.

MCRAE. Good show.

CLARKE. I also nearly got arrested.

MCRAE. Blimey. How?

CLARKE. Got lost. A place called – Berka?

MCRAE. Ah, well, aye . . .

CLARKE. I had to say it was for bunting.

MCRAE. Bunting?

CLARKE. And that I was on my way to find some white and blue.

McRae looks at Clarke.

MCRAE. Smart thinking. Where –

He goes back to his duplicating.

CLARKE. Downstairs. Now look here, Sarge –

MCRAE. (*At the duplicator.*) Let's keep it Alistair.

CLARKE. Now look here, Alistair . . .

He sees one of the leaflets, picks it up. It seems to be part of the general conspiracy.

What's this? Polish?

MCRAE. No, it's Greek. Polish is in English letters but without the vowels. (*Nodding at the leaflet.*) All greek to me.

Ballantine, having returned to pick up another bicycle, pops his head into the room.

BALLANTINE. Eh, mate. You a rider?

CLARKE. No. I got a jeep.

BALLANTINE. No, I mean, are you a cyclist?

CLARKE. No, I never learnt.

BALLANTINE. Well, no time like the present. There's thirty of us, go out, every Sunday morning. Any time you want a spin, you let me know.

He takes the second bike up the corridor.

MCRAE. (*With a nod towards Ballantine.*) Fanatic. (*Turning back to the leaflet.*) In fact, I have done Polish leaflets but I'm told they only work if you type them all in capitals . . .

CLARKE. Now, Alistair –

MCRAE. Now, comrade, what I'd like you to do now –

Ballantine returns for the last bike. He sees something down the corridor.

BALLANTINE. Eh. Cave, mate.

MCRAE. What?

Ballantine nods towards the stairhead and moves on. In what is clearly a practised manoeuvre, McRae takes the pile of duplicated Greek leaflets out of the tray, and puts them in a drawer. Then he puts another pile of already duplicated leaflets in the tray.

Bugger. I didn't reckon on himself till teatime.

Clarke is looking at the manoeuvre.

If there's one thing I can't do with, Nobby, is people being bloody unreliable.

Captain Carrington enters, with Clarke's kitbag. Clarke stands to attention. Carrington nods to him.

CARRINGTON. Airman. Sergeant.

MCRAE. Ah, sir. Your conference?

CARRINGTON. An utter washout.

MCRAE. Oh, I'm sorry, sir.

CARRINGTON. And this?

Carrington picks up a sheet from the tray. We see it. It's headed 'BTE Area 17: The Month at a Glance'. This is followed by a list of events.

MCRAE. Aircraftsman Clarke is kindly delivering a batch of these to Helio.

Slight pause.

That's his kitbag that you've got there, sir.

CARRINGTON. Oh? Right. Good show.

He gives Clarke the kitbag.

Well, thank you, Airman. Carry on.

Carrington goes and looks at files elsewhere in the office. Clearly, Clarke has no choice but to go with his kitbag.

CLARKE. (*Sotto voce.*) Um, Alistair –

McRae is scribbling an address on the back of a leaflet.

MCRAE. Um – eight o'clock. Tonight. Uh, comrade.

Nodding slightly at the two Other Ranks, Carrington takes the file out to the cuttings room.

CLARKE. (*Crossly.*) Well, I can't promise, Alistair.

Clarke goes out quickly, nearly bumping into Ballantine, who has come up from downstairs with another bike. Ballantine looks after Clarke.

BALLANTINE. So, what's up with your friend?

MCRAE. He's had a trying day.

As Ballantine moves towards the cuttings room with the bike, Carrington appears.

CARRINGTON. (*To Ballantine.*) Um, Staff . . .

Ballantine looks openly and frankly at his superior officer.

Interior. Heliopolis RAF camp: hangar. Day.

A trailer, laden with bits of a smashed-up Kittyhawk, is being pulled into the hangar. The Flight Sergeant, Beatty and other Riggers are watching.

BEATTY. Hey, wow.

He sees Clarke isn't there. He goes into the recess where Clarke sits, having read his letter.

Hey, Nob.

Clarke, distracted, stands.

CLARKE. I'm sorry.

Interior. Charlotte's apartment. Night.

Charlotte's apartment is fairly luxurious. It's full of books. In it at present are Charlotte herself, Wilson, Atterley, the Greek Ioannis, two or three other Greek soldiers, a young civilian woman, and the ATS Private who read Rosalind in the As You Like It *reading.*

Scissors and sewing materials are laid out on a table. McRae is standing by the window, looking out through the curtain. Silence. Everybody is waiting. McRae sees something.

MCRAE. It's him.

He goes to the door of the apartment and waits. A knock. McRae opens the door. Clarke stands there, with his booty.

Well, Comrade Clarke. 'Bout bloody time.

CLARKE. I'm sorry, I –

Clarke is almost pulled in, the door is shut. Immediately, activity. People quickly take the material and start cutting out red stars. The Greeks talking excitedly in Greek, Rosalind and Charlotte in French. Variously:

CHARLOTTE. (*In French.*) That's magnificent. We can do the entire army.

ROSALIND. (*In French.*) Now, who will organise this? Some big ones and some little ones.

CLARKE. A bit of a –

IOANNIS. (*In Greek.*) Look, ribbons. Ribbons are the best.

CLARKE. – a flap. Been at it since –

FIRST GREEK. (*In Greek.*) The towels are good, too.

CHARLOTTE. (*In French.*) Big ones for blouses, little ones for berets.

CLARKE. – this morning, actually.

CHARLOTTE. (*To Wilson.*) Steve, how long d'you think we have?

WILSON. Oh, till four a.m., about.

ATTERLEY. Or even a bit later.

SECOND GREEK. (*In Greek.*) We should have more scissors. It would be quicker.

FIRST GREEK. (*In French.*) Are there more scissors?

CHARLOTTE. (*In French, to Rosalind.*) I think there's a small pair in the lavatory.

> *Rosalind goes out in search of scissors. Clarke stands amid it all, looking confused.*

IOANNIS. (*In Greek.*) Make sure they're not too small. They must be seen from far away.

FIRST GREEK. (*In Greek, holding up a star.*) But these are for berets.

CLARKE. (*To McRae.*) Um, Alistair . . .

> *The Second Greek has put on an army blouse, to anticipate what it will look like. McRae announces:*

MCRAE. Nobby. Meet – elements of the Greek Royalist Army in exile, loyal of course to King George the Second, imperialistic lackey and protector of the late dictator General Metaxas –

> *Reaction. McRae takes a red star and holds it against the blouse of the Greek soldier:*

And now, meet cadres of the National Liberation Army, loyal to someone – and something – quite different.

> *Applause from those who understand.*

CLARKE. Don't get it.

MCRAE. Tomorrow morning, on parade, we effect the transformation. Today, white army. But on parade tomorrow morning – red.

Clarke still refusing to follow.

A demonstration. Like your bolshie buddy. Operation Cardinal.

Charlotte has loosely sewn a star on a beret. She puts it on the head of the Greek wearing the blouse.

CHARLOTTE. Voilà!

A Greek starts to sing the 'Internationale', in German.

Sh, shh.

Others join in, in various languages, as they work. Clarke makes for the door. Rosalind reappears with scissors.

ROSALIND. (*In French.*) Hey, they must be quiet. They'll be heard . . .

MCRAE. (*To Clarke.*) You going, Nobby?

CHARLOTTE. (*In French.*) Yes, Ioannis, for God's sake shut them up.

CLARKE. Yes.

IOANNIS. (*In Greek.*) Shh. Shh, shh. Comrades, be quiet, or we'll all be arrested.

MCRAE. So what's up, Nob?

The 'Internationale' dies away.

CLARKE. There's nothing up.

MCRAE. Don't give me that.

Pause; everyone is now aware.

CLARKE. Well, I suppose –

Slight pause.

MCRAE. Go on.

CLARKE. Well, it's just, I mean, you might say, this is very grand. And doubtless vaporous and inexpressible.

He breathes deeply.

But I wonder, I do wonder, what you think our people think about. The poor old bloody other ranks.

Slight pause.

Well, I'll tell you, Alistair. It's not the liberation of the subject peoples. And it's sure as hell not wages, prices or – 'Cos to be honest, your discussion group, I thought the best bit was the show you put on for the Brigadier.

He is about to stop, but he goes on.

I mean, my brother's in the – well, it doesn't matter, 'cos he isn't 'in the' now, 'cos he's got shot down and he's a prisoner.

CHARLOTTE. Oh, hard luck –

CLARKE. And the point is, he's like anybody. Like he's not stupid, but he don't read books much, and he'll get blotto when he's half the chance. But what I bet he'd like to know, is what it's going to be like when he gets home.

With a wave of his arm.

I mean, it's blokes like him you want to win the war.

Slight pause.

Now I'm going to find my lift. I'm tired. Good night.

He turns and goes out quickly. McRae flashes a look at Wilson. Pause. Then:

FIRST GREEK. What eez 'e talking? Airman?

WILSON. He is talking sense.

Slight pause.

MCRAE. What do you mean, Steve?

WILSON. I mean he's right. The discussion group is dull and we should be concerned about it.

ATTERLEY. Out of the mouths of babes . . .

WILSON. Exactly.

Interior. GHQ Public Relations: office. Day.

We hear Ballantine whistling. We see McRae's typewriter. He is typing an Agenda, on a stencil. What has been typed already:

Music for All 'Thinking Aloud'
Committee meeting, 2 November 1943
Agenda
1. Apologies.
2. Minutes of the last meeting.
3. Matters arising.

And what is being typed now:

4. Discussion: Future meetings.
   Attendance: How to increase.

We hear Ballantine's voice:

BALLANTINE. (*Out of vision.*) Hm. You know your problem, mate?

Ballantine is looking over McRae's shoulder. He is carrying a bicycle wheel.

MCRAE. (*Offhand.*) What's that?

BALLANTINE. Well, it's not that your meetings aren't, well, relevant. It's just they aren't, well, particularly entertaining.

McRae stops typing. He looks up at Ballantine. A note of sarcasm.

MCRAE. So. What do you suggest?

BALLANTINE. Well –

MCRAE. Jugglers? Burlesque? A Pierrot show?

BALLANTINE. No, mate. Just go out to Helwan. Check up on what the Springboks do out there.

MCRAE. The Springboks?

BALLANTINE. Mm.

Slight pause.

Here we all were, one Sunday morning, belting through the desert, bugger us, if we didn't ride straight into a full-scale bloody parliament.

MCRAE. A what?

BALLANTINE. Mock parliament. You know the sort of thing. Just, in this tent. There in the desert. Must have been fifty UDF types there. Sat round, debating this and that. Looked frightfully jolly. In fact, if we'd not been on a time trial, I'd have stayed.

Exterior. Desert. Day.

Clarke driving, Wilson map-reading, McRae in the back. They are not exactly lost, but not exactly sure where they are either. Two pyramids are coming into view.

WILSON. You know, apparently, the manuals, map-reading manuals, they isued at the start, completely useless.

He turns his map.

Not to mention, written in High Mandarin.

Clarke looks at Wilson.

Until, that is, they got in some bright Sergeant, done a bit of rambling, straightened it all out.

Clarke smiles to himself. Wilson sees one of the pyramids. Confidently:

Right. Splendid. Set course for that pyramid.

Wilson turns back to his map. Clarke has seen the other pyramid.

CLARKE. Uh – Steve . . .

WILSON. (*Benignly.*) Yes, what?

CLARKE. Which one?

Wilson looks at his map. His brow furrows. His friend McRae pats him on the shoulder.

MCRAE. Now don't you fret, son. Story of the war.

Interior. Tent. Late afternoon.

The Union Defence Force camp at Helwan: a large tent, with a makeshift bar at the side. The South African Forces Parliament is in session; it is a noisy, raucous affair. The Speaker of the Parliament is Lieutenant David Rubin.

FIRST SOUTH AFRICAN. May I ask the Minister of – whatever he's Minister of –

SECOND SOUTH AFRICAN. The Interior.

FIRST SOUTH AFRICAN. I beg his pardon, what his intention is in relation to the scandal of the alcoholic beverages available to the UDF troops in the Middle East –

SOUTH AFRICANS. Hear, hear!

THIRD SOUTH AFRICAN. You tell it, Barney!

FIRST SOUTH AFRICAN. I think particularly of that noxious beverage marketed under the title 'Stella Beer', or gyppo catpiss as it is more commonly known.

Cheers. McRae, Clarke and Wilson are watching this disgraceful spectacle.

RUBIN. Order.

SECOND SOUTH AFRICAN. I think I must point out that the Member for Bloemfontein –

FIRST SOUTH AFRICAN. Vereeniging, you fool –

SECOND SOUTH AFRICAN. Or whatever –

THIRD SOUTH AFRICAN. Come on, now, Jack, answer.

SOUTH AFRICANS. Answer, answer!

SECOND SOUTH AFRICAN. – is mistaken in his view . . .

RUBIN. I must ask honourable Members to bear in mind –

THIRD SOUTH AFRICAN. Answer the question!

SECOND SOUTH AFRICAN. Well, I am trying to . . .

RUBIN. – that if they do not make their remarks through the chair . . .

SOUTH AFRICANS. Resign! Resign!

RUBIN. . . . then they cannot be heard.

Once again, we see Clarke, Wilson and McRae, sitting on a bench, watching the Parliament. Wilson in particular looks very shocked.

Interior. Tent. Day.

Afterwards: at the bar, South Africans are drinking, joking and laughing. Lieutenant Rubin brings a tray of beers to a table, at which McRae, Wilson and Clarke are sitting.

RUBIN. (*Putting down his tray.*) It's all a bit vulgar and ribald, of course.

MCRAE. Well, aye.

RUBIN. (*Sitting.*) But it does wonders for morale. It gives them some kind of sense of what they're fighting for.

WILSON. Oh, yes. Indeed.

RUBIN. Now, me, I'm not concerned about the actual debates. It's the procedure that I'm fascinated by. Have you ever read Sir Thomas Erskine May, on Parliamentary Procedure?

THE BRITS. (*Variously.*) No, no.

RUBIN. Well, you should do so. That's if you want to take it seriously.

Wild laughter from the bar. The Brits look at each other.

WILSON. Oh, yes. We'd want to take it seriously.

RUBIN. Well, good. I wish you luck.

The men drink their beer.

WILSON. We'd want to take it very seriously indeed.

Interior. Music for All: Music Room. Evening.

On the stage of the Music Room, As You Like It *is being rehearsed. Act II, Scene V is leading on to Scene VI. At present then, Orlando, an imaginary*

Adam, the Producer and Duke Senior, Amiens and Lords waiting. No one is in costume or off the book; and indeed rehearsals are at a stage at which we will sense much stopping and starting. The Orlando actor is called Hugh Leslie, and is a Corporal.

LESLIE. Why, how now, Adam? No greater heart in thee?

> *He continues as we move to the back, where Neville Atterley sits, ostensibly waiting for his scene, but actually in conclave with Wilson and McRae. The rehearsal carries on in the background.*

WILSON. Well, the point is, Neville, that it might improve attendance.

ATTERLEY. Well, I think the problem *is*, that anything about discussion stinks of ABCA.

MCRAE. Nothing wrong with ABCA. All depends who does it.

ATTERLEY. Yes, I'm well aware that the Eighth Army more or less relied on Corporal McRae and his basic level course in Marxism for Boys –

MCRAE. But the point is that it isn't ABCA. The point is that it's voluntary. In leisure time.

ATTERLEY. Well, Alistair, I hate to say this, but –

MCRAE. Neville, I'm getting really browned off with –

WILSON. Now come on, turn it up, you two.

> *A pause, in which we can hear the Producer:*

PRODUCER. Right, into the next scene, from Orlando's exit. Stand by . . .

WILSON. My worry is, it'll be just entertainment.

ORLANDO. (*Pretending to carry 'Adam'.*) Come, I will bear thee to some shelter; and thou shalt not die for lack of a dinner . . .

ATTERLEY. There's nothing wrong with entertainment.

ORLANDO. . . . if there live any thing in this desert. Cheerly, good Adam!

ATTERLEY. Just as long as one remembers that it's all pretend.

WILSON. (*Still trying to convince himself.*) Look, the line is, unconditional support for the war effort.

MCRAE. Which this is.

WILSON. Defence of the progressive forces in each country.

MCRAE. Aye.

WILSON. And among our forces, maintenance at all costs of the highest levels of morale.

MCRAE. I rest my case.

ATTERLEY. Well, if you must . . .

Meanwhile, on stage.

DUKE SENIOR. I think he be transformed into a beast;
For I can nowhere find him like a man.
Go seek him, tell him I would speak with him.

AMIENS. He saves my labour by his own approach.

Atterley does not approach, but the Duke carries on, as the Producer goes to Atterley.

DUKE SENIOR. Why, how now, monsieur! What a life is this,
That your poor friends must woo your company?
What, you look merrily?

PRODUCER. (*To Atterley, with heavy irony.*) Now, Mr Atterley. There's a group of gentlemen, down here in the Forest of Arden, and they were wondering . . .

Atterley stands.

ATTERLEY. Ah, yes. The magic wood. Where everything is possible. Where are we?

PRODUCER. (*With feeling.*) A fool, a fool.

Atterley goes to the stage.

ATTERLEY. A fool, a fool! I met a fool i' th' forest,
A motley fool: a miserable world!

Wilson looks at his watch.

WILSON. We're late. We ought to scram.

MCRAE. Right then.

Interior. Music for All: Committee Room. Evening.

The 'Thinking Aloud' discussion group committee. Simpson, Garfield and Signalman Alf Jacobs, a Londoner, are already in session. McRae and Wilson enter.

GARFIELD. So, gentlemen, the next question, surely, is –

WILSON. I'm so sorry, Dr Garfield. Chaps.

SIMPSON. Uh, Steve, this is Alf Jacobs.

WILSON. (*Reaching out to shake hands.*) How d'you do.

SIMPSON. That's Councillor Alf Jacobs. Well, as was.

JACOBS. Whitechapel.

MCRAE. Could no be better.

   McRae and Wilson sit.

GARFIELD. – what you'd like to do. And who you'd like to do it.

SIMPSON. Nationalise the mines.

WILSON. Too easy.

MCRAE. What d'you mean?

WILSON. Well, you've got to let the opposition have a show.

SIMPSON. Do we expect an opposition?

   Pause.

WILSON. Well, I hope so.

SIMPSON. I'd have thought, there's bound to be some Common Wealth.

   McRae mimes machine-gunning. Wilson looks at him. He stops.

JACOBS. I wonder – what you'd all think of the Retail Trade.

   Slight pause.

I was in the Shop Workers' Union, and there was a lot of talk, before the war . . .

Pause.

SIMPSON. Sounds a grand idea. Does anyone object?

MCRAE. Well, my uncle runs a fag shop . . . No.

WILSON. We'd need to draft a bill.

JACOBS. I can do that.

WILSON. (*As he writes it down.*) And shouldn't we, as well, have some kind of leader of the Parliament, if we're going to have questions . . .

SIMPSON. Propose S. Wilson.

JACOBS. Seconded.

Wilson looks up.

WILSON. Uh, no.

Slight pause.

No, I'll be clerk. Or something like that.

Slight pause.

No, I thought of Jack.

MCRAE. Hear, hear.

SIMPSON. Well, I –

WILSON. (*Writing it down.*) Elected by acclaim.

JACOBS. Well, then, that's it.

End-of-meeting atmosphere. Pens being capped, papers gathered, people standing.

JACOBS. Steve contacts his chum at Helwan for the Speaker, I draw up the bill and we all think of questions.

GARFIELD. Um, gentlemen . . . There is one final point.

Stillness. Anyone who has stood up, sits.

WILSON. Yes, Dr Garfield?

GARFIELD. It's a matter that we should, at least, consider.

He lays open a booklet, and reads from it:

'No officer or soldier, or member of Queen Alexandra's Imperial Military Nursing Service . . .'

Slight reaction.

'. . . is permitted to take any active part in the affairs of any political organisation or party, either by acting as a member of the candidate's selection committee, or . . . etcetera etcetera in furtherance of the political purposes of any such organisation or party, until he or she has retired, resigned or been discharged.' King's Regulations. 541, A.

Pause.

SIMPSON. Oh, come on –

WILSON. Surely it's not –

MCRAE. As Neville says, it's all pretend –

JACOBS. Well, yes. It's acting.

Slight pause.

Isn't it? I mean, wouldn't it be like charging an actor playing Macbeth for murder? I mean, they couldn't stop it, could they?

GARFIELD. Well, I can't think that they *would*.

Interior. Music for All: lobby. Evening.

Major Trapnell of the Army Education Corps goes to the Admissions Desk, taking money from his pocket.

TRAPNELL. One, please.

He looks at the price list and sees it's three piastres for ORs and five for officers. He puts down five piastres and takes his ticket.

Interior. Music for All: corridor. Evening.

Trapnell marches along the corridor to the entrance of the Music Room. On the door are McRae and Nobby Clarke. There is much bustle, servicemen and women going into the first session of the Parliament. Trapnell arrives at the door just as McRae admits a pair of naval ratings.

TRAPNELL. Good evening, Sergeant. This is the mock parliament?

MCRAE. That's right, sir.

Clarke gives Trapnell a duplicated sheet.

TRAPNELL. (*Looking at his sheet.*) Thank you, Airman. And so, what are you planning to expropriate this evening?

MCRAE. Oh, just the retail trade tonight, sir.

TRAPNELL. Oh, I see. There's more?

MCRAE. Well, ultimately, more or less the lot, I'd think, sir.

TRAPNELL. Yes. I see.

He goes in. Clarke to the people entering, giving as many as he can a duplicated sheet:

CLARKE. Get your order papers *here*.

Interior. Music for All: Music Room. Evening.

The final 'Members' are coming in. The Music Room is not full, but there are nearly 200 people present. The committee is largely on the front row on the left. On the stage, the Speaker's chair. In front of the stage, the Clerk's desk and chair. Both the Speaker's chair and the Clerk's are presently empty. Wilson stands with Rubin at the side. Wilson is staggered by the numbers.

RUBIN. Well, it's nine o'clock. Should we make a start?

WILSON. Uh, yes. Why not.

He recovers his composure, and goes to the Clerk's desk, passing Simpson and Atterley on the 'front bench'. Simpson grins encouragingly. Wilson bangs his desk for silence.

WILSON. Everybody rise.

Everybody does, eventually, but one or two with a chuckle, and a push. Rubin enters carrying books. He sits in the Speaker's chair.

Honourable Members may sit.

A MEMBER. (*To another.*) 'Honourable Members'!

RUBIN. Good evening, and welcome to the first session of the Music for All Parliament.

A smattering of applause.

I think they are on the order paper, but I would like to begin by the Clerk reading the rules of procedure and debate.

WILSON. Yes. Certainly. (*He reads.*) '1. Members must address their remarks to the Chair, using the term "Mr Speaker" or "Sir". 2. Members must not refer to other Members by name, but as "the Minister" or "the Honourable Member" or "the Honourable and Gallant Member" for officers.' (*He looks up.*) In the parliamentary manner. (*He reads on.*) '3. Honourable Members should avoid personal allusions and unparliamentary expressions.'

Laughter. Wilson gets through the rest – particularly the dangerous rule on applause – with dispatch, though there are reactions.

'4. Approval will be signified by the use of the expression "Hear, hear" or by clapping of hands. 5. No Member may leave or take his seat in the House without bowing to the chair. And, six, Mr Speaker's ruling on all matters is final.'

RUBIN. Thank you, Mr Clerk. The first item of business today is questions to – Yes?

For an uppity Australian Member is on his feet already.

UPPITY MEMBER. On a point of information, Mr Speaker?

RUBIN. Yes?

UPPITY MEMBER. Could you give us an example of an 'unparliamentary expression' that we shouldn't use?

Laughter. Rubin opens a fat tome.

RUBIN. With pleasure. According to the noted authority, Sir Thomas Erskine May, the following expressions have in the past been deemed to be unparliamentary: (*He reads.*) 'Villains', 1875, 'impertinence', 1879, 'gross calumny', 1889, 'ruffianism, hypocrites, and pharisees –'

Interior. Music for All: corridor. Evening.

McRae and Clarke are waiting for latecomers.

CLARKE. Well, then?

MCRAE. Well what?

CLARKE. Is it a bigger crowd than you expected?

MCRAE. (*Transparent.*) What? Oh, no . . . (*He suddenly remembers.*) Oh, bloody hell. I've got to ask a question. Would you hold the fort?

He rushes in.

CLARKE. Ar. Sure. Why not.

Interior. Music for All: Music Room. Evening.

Simpson is taking questions. Atterley is asking the first question. Wilson notes with relief that McRae – who is to ask the second question – is hurrying down to the 'front bench'.

ATTERLEY. Thank you, Mr Speaker. May I ask the Prime Minister whether His Majesty's Government will consider adding Naafi employees to their list of war criminals, with a view to their eventually being brought to trial at the cessation of hostilities?

Laughter.

SIMPSON. The answer to that question, sir, is 'No'. The Government is conscious that many complaints have been forwarded on this topic, but they consider that the real root of the trouble lies in the fact that the consumers are not represented on the Naafi local management, and if the Bill being presented this evening becomes law, it is felt that Naafi services will be considerably ameliorated.

RUBIN. (*Reading from a list.*) The Member for Lanark.

McRae asks his question.

MCRAE. And will the Prime Minister inform the House if any steps are being taken to bring home men who have been in the Middle East for more than twenty-five years?

Laughter.

SIMPSON. Well, now. H.M. Government has always viewed with sympathy the desires of those men serving abroad to rejoin their families . . .

Laughter. Simpson catches it.

. . . but perhaps the time has come to move on to the main debate.

RUBIN. The President of the Board of Trade.

Jacobs rises and begins. A little nervously to begin with.

JACOBS. Mr Speaker, I rise to introduce the Retail Trade (Nationalisation) Bill before this House.

Interior. Music for All: corridor. Evening.

Clarke, alone in the corridor, glances at his watch. He decides there will be no more latecomers now and enters the Music Room.

Interior. Music for All: Music Room. Evening.

We enter the Music Room with Clarke. Jacobs' speech is continuing. We sense that this is going on a bit, and is pretty dry stuff.

JACOBS. . . . a National Distribution Board, on which will sit consumers' representatives, and unions, together with persons of the necessary, the necessary administrative experience. And of course there will be in addition a full network of regional . . .

Interior. Music for All: Music Room. Evening.

Jacobs continues to continue. People are gazing about and nodding off.

JACOBS. . . . it shall not, however, be accepted that the Government shall necessarily pay compensation at the current market value, but it is accepted that the Government will guarantee to individual proprietors . . .

Clarke, standing at the back, yawns.

Interior. Music for All: Music Room. Evening.

Jacobs is finishing. There is a slight revival of interest; the House is sympathetic with the meat of what Jacobs has to say.

JACOBS. . . . in the interests of the workers in the retail trade, the housewife and indeed the nation in the doubtless arduous but nonetheless we trust both challenging and ultimately prosperous years that lie ahead.

He sits. A moment before the applause – which has that slightly forced feel when people are keener on the content than on the delivery. Then there is silence.

RUBIN. The Bill is now open to debate.

Pause.

I am hoping to, uh, catch a Member's eye.

Pause. McRae and Atterley are each gesturing the other to intervene. Finally, an RAF Corporal puts his hand up. He is Douglas Richardson. His delivery is a little uncertain.

RICHARDSON. Mr Speaker, the proposer has tried to argue that there is no alternative to his proposals to create a centralised state bureaucracy, which would own and control every shop and market. Well, there *is* an alternative. It is common ownership, This is not a matter of the secretaries of the big unions sitting on a (*He checks a note.*) National Distribution whatever. It is a matter of the workers themselves controlling the fruits of their labours. It is in essence a Christian principle that we in Common Wealth have always fought for.

Richardson sits. Again, the applause feels a little forced. An army Captain, Graham Castle, who has been watching Richardson closely, comes over to him. There is a pause before, in desperation, McRae puts his hand up.

RUBIN. The – I believe, the Scottish Member.

McRae stands as Castle puts his hand out to Richardson.

CASTLE. Castle, AEC. Well done.

Richardson looks up, smiles, shakes Castle's hand, as:

MCRAE. Indeed so, Mr Speaker. I merely rise to say, it is interesting, once again, to note that what 'common ownership' actually means in practice is hostility towards the idea of democratic planning on the one hand, and the trade union movement on the other.

CASTLE. Nonsense!

McRae gives a rhetorical shrug, as he sits. Another pause. Then Trapnell's hand is up.

RUBIN. The Honourable and Gallant Member in the third row on the right . . .

TRAPNELL. Mr Speaker, it's very good that at last we have some opposition to this Bill, even if it appears to consist thus far of a desultory scrap between two different types of socialist. I think we all know that the basic disagreement between the Common Wealth party and Labour is that Common Wealth doesn't believe in the electoral truce, and because the major parties do, it has managed to win, I think, one by-election.

RICHARDSON. That's not the only difference!

RUBIN. Order.

TRAPNELL. No, there are others: Common Wealth believes in common ownership, whatever that may mean, Labour in state control, and we know quite well what *that* means. I suspect, in practice, they'd look very much the same.

Castle smiles, shaking his head.

In the case of the retail trade, they'd both look like the Naafi.

A moment before the audience gets it. A hum of concurrence, but also of disagreement. Trapnell is effectively – and perhaps intentionally – winding them up.

Or indeed another institution with which we are familiar. I would like Honourable Members, Mr Speaker, to cast their minds back, and to remember quite the dullest, least imaginative, and usually worst-stocked store in any High Street. Yes, that's right. The Co-op.

The pros and antis are getting more bullish. The Labour front bench look at each other in concern: this is rather good.

And what we have seen, quite properly, quite understandably, in wartime, is more like the Co-op and the Naafi than the High Street of the pre-war days. But what do we want afterwards? When things are back to normal? Well, I'd say, we'd want things – back to normal.

Continued response.

Because for all the good intentions, without competition, without choice, you end up with either the black market or the ration book, either corruption or the queue. So, Mr Speaker, I would urge the House to vote for choice, to vote for the real interests of the housewife and the worker – and against this motion.

He sits, quietly pleased with himself. The response is strong in both directions – though numerically, there are more against what he has said than for. Rubin looks out from his chair on a sea of hands.

RUBIN. Um, the Member – yes, I think, the Member in the naval uniform . . .

An angry Wren stands, pointing at herself, questioningly.

Yes, please, miss, you.

ANGRY WREN. Well, Mr Chairman, I'd just like to say, that I've never heard such a load of – such a – well, it may not be a parliamentary expression, but such a load of downright balderdash in all my life.

There are cheers.

And I'd like to ask the – what is it, the Honourable and Gallant Member, if he realises that before the war, it was quite 'normal' for most children to walk around in second-hand or third-hand boots? And that the first bacon ration – I remember this – was *more* than most people had before?

Applause.

And when he talks about the *queues*. And *choice*. Well, I think that he's forgotten that before the war a lot of people, it was normal for a lot of people to spend quite a time in queues – dole queues –

OTHERS. Hear, hear!

ANGRY WREN. – under his so-called free enterprise, and they didn't have much choice about it neither!

She sits, to applause. Rubin points to a Flight Sergeant, Geoffrey Carter.

CARTER. Yes, Mr Speaker, it does stick in one's craw a little to hear the old system praised so fulsomely by one of its obvious beneficiaries.

Trapnell looks quizzically over at Carter.

But I suppose it's par for the course – when we still have officers writing to *The Times* regretting that nowadays they're commissioning 'just anybody'.

Reaction. McRae is going over to Atterley.

And how many people here who've been up for commission found themselves being asked where they played cricket? Who they hunt with?

Laughter. During which:

MCRAE. D'you know this character?

ATTERLEY. No. Don't think he's one of ours.

MCRAE. I bet you anything, he's Common Wealth.

CARTER. Well, I'll tell you who I hunt with. I hunt with the only group that's actually standing up against the vested interests and the old school tie.

MCRAE. I told you.

CARTER. Common Wealth.

He sits, to applause. Rubin points to an RAF officer.

RUBIN. Um – the Honourable and Gallant - no, in front of you, the Flight . . .

Flight Lieutenant Trelawney concludes it's him:

TRELAWNEY. What, me? Right. Me.

He stands.

It is – Mr Speaker, it does go against the grain for me to agree so fully with the socialists – by politics I'm Liberal . . .

A certain amount of reaction.

. . . but before the war I was a member of a health board, and if I may say so in that area a return to normal would be to go back to a state of shame.

Applause. He has a notebook.

Nearly half the population medically undernourished. Only half the population covered by health insurance. Waiting lists for operations in six figures, and that's *before* the war. Well, that may be normal in the Tory book, but it's – forgive me, ladies – it's a damn disgrace in mine.

He sits, to applause. The forest of hands is growing no thinner.

RUBIN. Yes, you, you, you . . . then, you . . .

Interior. Music for All: Music Room. Evening.

There are still many speakers but Rubin has decided to call it time.

RUBIN. We have now reached the point of the division. Can tellers please take their places.

One of the tellers is Clarke.

Can I see all those in favour of the second reading?

A majority. The tellers counting.

Um – I think – all those against?

A minority.

I declare the motion carried overwhelmingly. The session is adjourned.

Applause. Rubin and Wilson stand.

WILSON. All stand.

All do. Rubin goes out. As soon as he is gone, the Labour Members celebrate, pumping each other's hands, particularly Jacobs', and slapping each other on the back. Trapnell comes over to them.

TRAPNELL. Congratulations, gentlemen. I'm Trapnell, AEC.

Trapnell puts his hand out in a generalised manner. Wilson shakes it.

WILSON. Well, thank you.

TRAPNELL. Bill well drafted. Clever speech. Not absolutely sure they were voting for the motion, but . . . The whole thing, most impressive.

SIMPSON. Thanks.

TRAPNELL. I must admit, a bit surprised, about the numbers . . . But, you've clearly touched a nerve. Well done.

He smiles and leaves.

MCRAE. You patronising bastard.

ATTERLEY. Well, I think he may be right. About the motion.

MCRAE. Well, he's still a patronising bastard.

Trapnell passes Castle and Richardson.

TRAPNELL. Well, hallo, Graham.

CASTLE. Major.

TRAPNELL. Pretty clear who's running this show, is it not?

Trapnell walks on. We stay with Castle and Richardson.

CASTLE. So where are you billeted, Douglas?

RICHARDSON. Kas Fareet. We've a group of five or six out there.

CASTLE. CW?

RICHARDSON. That's right.

Carter approaches.

CARTER. Good evening, comrades. Carter. Just up from Kenya. Base Accounts. (*Before Richardson or Castle can react.*) Yes, I know. Jammy sod.

Back to the Labour group. Rubin appears.

RUBIN. Now, gentlemen, I suspect you might have cause for celebration.

MCRAE. Aye. Aye, right.

Interior. Music for All: Music Room. Evening.

A little later. The room is empty. Wilson is tidying up his papers. Clarke stands at the back. He comes forward.

CLARKE. So what d'you think? Will you hold another one?

WILSON. Oh, yes. It's been a huge success.

Slight pause.

I mean, I'd thought, around . . . I thought we'd be lucky to get fifty.

Clarke smiles.

Any news about your brother?

CLARKE. No. I don't think . . . No.

Pause. Wilson smiles, and is about to go out with Clarke. But something is on his mind, and he stops. Clarke looks questioningly at him.

WILSON. You see, I thought there'd be – the stuff about the need for full employment and state medicine, you know, the stuff that no one disagrees with . . . But what I'd not expected . . . Somehow, a sense of . . . something I can't put my finger on.

Clarke doesn't know what to say.

Well. Perhaps we shouldn't be surprised. Have more faith in the masses.

CLARKE. And in Lawrence of Arabia.

Wilson looks quizzically at Clarke. Then he gets it.

WILSON. Indeed.

Wilson goes to the exit, meeting McRae coming in.

MCRAE. Now, aren't you fellows coming?

WILSON. Yes. Yes, certainly.

He gestures Clarke through, remaining a moment with McRae.

We should put that lad on the committee.

McRae looks at Wilson, a smile playing round his mouth.

Yes. Full marks, Alistair.

Interior. Officers' Mess bar. Day.

Trapnell has bought Pugh a copy of the Egyptian Gazette, *at which Pugh is looking. We see the headline:*

'*Cairo Forces Parliament Takes Over High St.
First meeting attracts 200.*'

PUGH. Well, a great success all round, then, John.

TRAPNELL. Well, I'm very pleased you feel that way, sir.

PUGH. Absolutely. Great advertisement. For ABCA and the Corps.

TRAPNELL. Particularly, as . . .

PUGH. Mm?

TRAPNELL. I've been asked to serve on their committee. The group that organises things.

PUGH. Oh, good idea.

TRAPNELL. And in fact, as well, I have a Captain, Graham Castle, and they've asked him too.

PUGH. Yes, well, I've no objection.

TRAPNELL. Thank you, sir.

Pause. Pugh reads the report in the paper.

PUGH. Standing Orders. Honourable Members. The President of the Board of Trade. They're very keen, aren't they, to make this like the real thing.

TRAPNELL. Yes, I think they're even keener, sir –

Pugh looks at Trapnell.

– to make the real thing like this.

We hear the voice of the present-day McRae.

MCRAE. (*Voice over.*) For me, the crucial thing was that you had the blokes supposed to take the orders, and they're working out how to give the orders.

Interior. Room. Day.

Close-up of the present-day Alistair McRae, in his late sixties, being interviewed.

MCRAE. And what that led them on to was the notion that the Britain they came home to afterwards, that it needn't be the same as the one they left behind. That it could be changed, and they could be the ones to change it.

Slight pause.

Well, as you can imagine. Bound to cause a stir.

He grins.

Closing titles of Episode One.

Episode Two

Interior. Room. Day.

We see the present-day Steve Wilson, being interviewed, in close-up.

WILSON. Now you must remember, the war put an end to a lot of deference. You had shop assistants, clippies – usually women and girls, obviously – who'd been, well, quite subservient before the war. But now they felt themselves to be as good as anyone.

Exterior. Egyptian Desert, December 1943. Morning.

A figure is bicycling on a road across the desert. He signals - otiosely - and makes a right turn. We hear the voice of the present-day Wilson:

WILSON. (*Voice over.*) And that applied in the services as well, where, in reality, rank didn't cut much ice at all. If anything, it was the NCOs who really ran the show. And our Parliament, which had no rank, was a kind of symbol of that fact. And one can understand, one can see how the brass might feel the thing to be a threat.

Exterior. Heliopolis RAF camp: main gate. Morning.

Staff Sergeant Ballantine cycles up to the barrier. The Guard looks out of the Guardhouse. Ballantine makes a little pantomime.

BALLANTINE. Um – I've a chitty somewhere . . .

The Guard shrugs, raises the barrier, and Ballantine rides through.

Interior. Heliopolis RAF camp: tent. Morning.

Four men sleeping in a tent, bedecked with Christmas decorations. A voice from outside:

BALLANTINE. (*Out of vision.*) Hallo! Halloa! Anybody there?

Beatty stumbles out of bed and pulls back the flap of the tent. Ballantine stands there. He smiles cheerfully.

Good morrow, friend.

BEATTY. Uh – Sarge?

BALLANTINE. Bill. Nobby?

Beatty gets his mind round this.

BEATTY. Ar.

Ballantine hands over a letter.

BALLANTINE. Ta ta for now.

Beatty watches through the flap.

Exterior. Heliopolis RAF camp: outside tent. Morning.

Ballantine gets on his bike.

Interior. Heliopolis RAF camp: tent. Morning.

Beatty turns back into the tent, takes the note over to Clarke's bed.

BEATTY. Hey. Nob?

Clarke wakes.

CLARKE. Yes, what?

BEATTY. Some – army sarge.

He gives Clarke the letter. Blearily, Clarke opens it. The note is on GHQ notepaper, but takes the form of a cod formal invitation: 'The Forces of Progress request the Pleasure of the Company of Mr Nobby Clarke at the meeting of the Music for All Parliamentary Committee, to be held at 8.30 of the clock on Friday 31 December 1943, Dress Informal but Essential', signed 'Alistair'.

Interior. GHQ Public Relations: office. Day.

McRae and Ballantine's office, GHQ Public Relations. Sound of typing, and a carol being whistled. We start with a noticeboard, with the Egyptian Gazette *story about the Parliament clipped and displayed, with its headline:*

'Cairo Forces Parliament Takes Over High St.
First meeting attracts 200.'

Then Ballantine – the whistler – pins on a huge cutting about his cycling club, with several pictures of a cycle race. We see that it is McRae who is typing away, and we take in Christmas decorations.

BALLANTINE. Well, there it is, mate. Gyp Gazette. The Centre Spread. Thirty inches, I'd say, wouldn't you?

Ballantine looks over to McRae. McRae is typing a document headed Inheritance Restriction Bill.

Oh, by the by, I bunged your secret missive into Nobby What's-'is-name at Helio. Six twenty and the bugger's still asleep.

Ballantine goes to McRae and takes a desultory look at what he is typing. Presently, this is the following:

'*Of the 6 members, 3 shall be elected by the TUC, one by the Co-operative Movement, one shall represent the Ministry of Agriculture.*'

McRae looks up at Ballantine, as if to say, (a) don't look over what I'm doing and (b) stop jabbering. Ballantine moves back to look at his cuttings.

If not six twenty-five.

    Captain Carrington comes in, briskly.

CARRINGTON. Right, chaps. Just down the wire. Announced command for the invasion. It's Eisenhower SAC, Air Marshal Tedder deputy, and Monty with the British armies on the ground.

    The two Sergeants look at him.

BALLANTINE. Invasion, sir?

CARRINGTON. Yes. The invasion.

    Slight pause.

Second front. Or third front. France. The European fortress. The Invasion.

MCRAE. What, on Christmas Eve?

CARRINGTON. No. No, it's . . . (*Desperately.*) The command of the invasion.

BALLANTINE. (*Comfortingly.*) We'll prepare a press release.

CARRINGTON. *Thank* you, Staff.

    He looks at the two men, who clearly are not going to do this immediately. Ballantine looks at his cutting, McRae carries on typing. Carrington goes out. Pause. Ballantine goes to his desk.

BALLANTINE. So, what are you doing?

    McRae looks up.

MCRAE. I am formulating a blueprint for the new Jerusalem, Staff Sergeant.

BALLANTINE. Ah. I see.

Interior. Music for All: Music Room. Evening.

A rehearsal of As You Like It*: Act II, Scene VII. The Producer watches.*

Atterley playes Jacques and Corporal Hugh Leslie plays Orlando. He enters with sword drawn.

LESLIE. Forbear, and eat no more.

ATTERLEY. Why, I have eat none yet.

LESLIE. Nor shall not till necessity be served.

Atterley notices that McRae has come in at the back and is waving and pointing at his watch.

ATTERLEY. (*A little offhand.*) Of what kind should this cock come of?

DUKE SENIOR. What would you have? Your gentleness shall force
More than your force move us to gentleness.

Atterley realises he is late, and looks about. Among other actors, Rosalind is sitting in the wings, perhaps going through her words with someone else.

LESLIE. I almost die for food, and let me have it.

As Duke Senior speaks, Atterley goes to Rosalind, thrusts his script at her, points her to the stage, and hurries out, pointing at his watch towards the exasperated Producer.

DUKE SENIOR. Sit down and feed, and welcome to our table.

LESLIE. Speak you so gently? Pardon me, I pray you.
I thought that all things . . .

Everyone is looking at Atterley hurrying out, or at Rosalind, who has tried to sidle into Atterley's place. The Producer, angry, waves Leslie on:

. . . had been savage here.

Interior. Music for All: Committee Room. Afternoon.

The Committee of the Parliament has been expanded to include representatives of the other parties. Present are Simpson, Clarke, Jacobs, Wilson, Garfield, Trapnell, Castle, Carter, Richardson and Trelawney; McRae and Atterley are just arriving. The whole thing is rather artificially formal at the moment. Clarke is very nervous about his new role. Garfield calls the meeting to order.

GARFIELD. Now, gentlemen . . .

The meeting comes to order.

Now, gentlemen. We'd like to welcome Major Trapnell and Captain Castle of the AEC, uh, Douglas Richardson, who as we know backs Common Wealth, and Frank Trelawney, who has agreed, at very short notice, to represent the Liberal interest.

TRELAWNEY. How do you do.

ALL OLD HANDS. (*Variously.*) Hallo, how d'you do, evening, welcome aboard, etc.

GARFIELD. And, um, we also have with us Geoffrey Carter, who is I gather known to some of you, and who's just arrived back with RAF Base Accounts from Kenya –

SIMPSON. Jammy sod.

A little laughter.

GARFIELD. – and is also a Common Wealth supporter.

ATTERLEY. Even jammier.

A little more laughter.

GARFIELD. – and, Nobby Clarke, from Heliopolis. Now, tonight's main business is the next meeting of the Parliament, to be held – next Wednesday, January the fifth. Steve.

WILSON. Well, following the last meeting, Alf and I – Alf's becoming a dab hand at this – have cobbled together an initial draft for a Bill. (*Handing round copies.*) I've copies of it here, which we would propose proposing.

TRAPNELL. (*Reading.*) 'Inheritance Restriction Bill.'

JACOBS. Well, it's more, inheritance elimination, if the truth be told.

TRAPNELL. You stagger me.

That comes out heavier than intended. Slight hiatus. Then:

WILSON. And it was thought, also, that it might be an idea to put forward some other, briefer motions, to give some variety to the proceedings, and it struck us, having received a very large number of submitted questions, that some of those might form the basis of short Bills. That's the ones that don't concern the Naafi.

A little laughter.

TRAPNELL. And these – proposals, came from people who attended the first meeting?

WILSON. Yes.

ATTERLEY. There's been a lot of interest.

MCRAE. But no unexpected.

Trapnell looks at McRae.

I mean, *we* were no 'surprised' the meeting pulled in upward of 200.

SIMPSON. No.

Trapnell raises his eyebrows a shade. Wilson plays with the top of his pen.

TRELAWNEY. And would it not . . .

This comes out a little louder than intended. Everyone looks at him.

Um, couldn't the, um, leading faction appoint spokesmen. Even 'ministers'. To deal with matters in their area of responsibility.

Castle, who has some sense of the hidden agendas operating in this sticky meeting, says drily:

CASTLE. Just like the real thing.

Interior. Music for All: Committee Room. Evening.

End of the meeting. The only people left in the room are Wilson and John Trapnell.

TRAPNELL. Well, Wilson. A good Christmas?

WILSON. Yes. Yes, thank you, sir.

TRAPNELL. Though I don't suppose you fellows are that keen –

WILSON. Oh, I don't think we'll abolish Christmas, sir. Certainly not in the first year or two.

Trapnell smiles.

But now you mention it, I think I'm less interested in the old year than the new.

TRAPNELL. Of course.

Slight pause.

Look, Wilson. I can read you. You don't want brass hats muscling in.

Wilson looks at Trapnell.

But you know the situation here. Émigré armies, split from top to tail, on whether they're to be, well, white or red. You know, the Poles, the Yugoslavs. The Greeks.

Slight pause.

And I'm sure that by comparison, that ABCA, the whole army education racket, it must seem pretty milk and water. But we can't build your new world in a country cracked in two.

Slight pause.

WILSON. Yes, I see how you might feel that, sir.

TRAPNELL. Which is why I do believe that you – that we must all – be treated, treat each other, not as cannon fodder, like the last time, but as citizens in uniform. And why I shall continue, quite inadequately, no doubt, to do my job.

Wilson says nothing. Trapnell gives up for the moment.

TRAPNELL. A happy new year, Steve.

Interior. Officers' Mess. Night.

At the Officers' New Year Dinner. In attendance are the General commanding, the Brigadier, a Signals Colonel, Another Colonel, Pugh and Trapnell.

GENERAL. The King.

All stand.

ALL. The King.

They drink and sit.

GENERAL. The Empire.

Interior. Music for All: Pergola Café. Night.

The Common Wealthers – including Carter, Richardson and Castle – are celebrating in the Music for All pergola café. Christmas decorations are still up.

CARTER. To the Red Army.

ALL. To the Red Army.

RICHARDSON. To a Britain of equality, good fellowship and justice.

Interior. Charlotte's apartment. Night.

Wilson, McRae and Atterley are celebrating at Charlotte's apartment. The ATS who plays Rosalind, and the Greek partisan, Ioannis, are among the others.

CHARLOTTE. To the liberation of the European peoples from the fascist yoke.

ALL. The liberation of the European peoples from the fascist yoke.

WILSON. To the resistance forces of the subject nations.

Interior. Heliopolis RAF camp: Naafi. Late evening.

A group of airmen – including Beatty – are drinking and singing 'Roll Out the Barrel'. Beatty realises that Clarke is not among them and goes and looks for him. Clarke is sitting apart, drinking beer and reading an ABCA pamphlet on the Beveridge Report. Beatty discovers his friend.

BEATTY. Eh, shape up, Nob. It's nearly Old Lang's Time.

Clarke sits up, closes the pamphlet.

CLARKE. I'm sorry.

BEATTY. Eh, what's up? You ain't half looking flaked.

CLARKE. Oh, nothing.

BEATTY. Hey, 'tin't about your brother?

CLARKE. No.

Pause.

BEATTY. It must be something. New Year's Eve.

Slight pause.

CLARKE. Well. If you really want to know. Today, I was appointed Minister of Labour.

Interior. Music for All: Music Room. Evening.

The Parliament is in session. About 200 people are present. Rubin in the chair; Wilson as Clerk; McRae, Clarke, Simpson and Jacobs as the 'government'; Atterley nearby, sitting next to 'Rosalind'; Castle, Carter and Richardson; Trelawney; Garfield and Trapnell. We start with Clarke, who is making last-minute adjustments to his notes, in consultation with his ABCA pamphlet. Meanwhile, Trapnell is looking fixedly at McRae.

MCRAE. In broad outline, our purpose will be to create a system in which each child will be guaranteed the education most suitable for the development of his full capacities, irrespective of his social origin.

Richardson whispers to Carter. Thereby, he actually misses some of the substance of McRae's continued speech:

To this end, it will be made illegal for anyone to set up or maintain schools or colleges outside the state system. Maintenance grants will be provided for children in post-primary education, and transport provided where necessary. The school leaving age will be raised to sixteen immediately.

ATTERLEY. (*To Rosalind.*) 'L go through on the nod, I'd think.

McRae sits. Richardson already has his hand up.

RUBIN. The Honourable Member from the Common Wealth –

RICHARDSON. Mr Speaker. Can I ask the Minister, if he plans to do anything about the scandal, the immoral scandal, of the public schools?

A buzz.

MCRAE. The answer to that is that it goes without saying. In fact, I think I said it nonetheless.

Nods from the socialist group.

The Honourable Member's attention must have been elsewhere. He was probably concentrating on his Christian principles.

Delight among the socialist group. Richardson sits, flummoxed. Carter scratches his ear. Rubin looks at his list, as Wilson looks at his watch.

RUBIN. The Minister of Labour.

Clarke breathes deeply and stands. Wilson, realising the time, turns and whispers urgently to Rubin. At the same time:

ROSALIND. Who is this boy?

ATTERLEY. Oh, Bobby? Cobby? One of Alistair's.

Clarke begins:

CLARKE. Uh, Mr Speaker, um –

But Rubin interrupts:

RUBIN. I beg your pardon. I am informed that as time is pressing we must move on to the main debate.

CLARKE. Uh – right.

He sits – relieved but a little disappointed.

RUBIN. The Minister of Planning.

Trapnell is looking very irritated. McRae, Wilson, Jacobs and finally Rosalind attract the attention of the Minister of Planning.

ATTERLEY. What? Oh, me.

He stands, finding his notes.

Mr Speaker. I rise to introduce the Government's Inheritance Restriction Bill –

Trapnell looks pointedly to Garfield.

– before this House. This Bill has a single purpose. It is to eliminate totally the present system by which the children of the wealthy have a huge head-start in life, due to nothing more than an accident of birth.

Interior. Music for All: Committee Room. Afternoon.

The Parliament Committee in session. Jacobs, Simpson, Wilson, McRae, Castle, Clarke, Carter, Garfield, Trelawney, Richardson and Trapnell, who speaks from notes.

TRAPNELL. Point one. I am sure that we all wish our proceedings, mock or not, to be conducted with the seriousness that behoves a discussion of issues that are of vital importance to the future of our country. I note, however, that several such issues went by, if not through, as I think the Minister of Planning aptly put it, on the nod.

He looks round the table. No Atterley.

Where is the Minister of Planning?

People look round. Shrugs.

CLARKE. He's practising a play.

TRAPNELL. What?

WILSON. *As You Like It.*

Trapnell looks at Wilson. Then:

TRAPNELL. Two. I am deeply disturbed, and I'm sure I'm not alone, that those perfunctorily treated matters arose out of questions to ministers which were largely written by those ministers themselves, their friends and comrades.

CLARKE. Oh . . .

He looks round. It's clear this is true. McRae makes a gesture: Don't push this.

TRAPNELL. Point three. In general, it's my view this Parliament's a ramp.

Pause.

It is being deliberately manipulated by a clique, what Frank rightly called a leading faction, though one might better call it leading cadre, not in the interests of free discussion and debate, but in order to provide a propaganda platform for ideas that in my view are not those of the vast majority of troops in Cairo.

Outrage. Variously:

SIMPSON. Oh, now, come on –

JACOBS. I wouldn't bet on that one.

CARTER. If it is a ramp, it's a damn sight –

TRELAWNEY. I really think that is a bit unfair –

SIMPSON. There's a lot of work put into this, you know –

MCRAE. Doing AEC's job for it, I'd say.

As it dies:

WILSON. Well, I'm sorry that you feel like that. I wonder if anyone agrees?

Slight pause.

From any of the other parties?

MCRAE. Like perhaps, on moral grounds.

Castle and Richardson look annoyed but don't intervene.

WILSON. Well, it does appear . . .

Trapnell gathers his papers.

TRAPNELL. I've said my piece. I'm sorry, Dr Garfield.

He stands.

GARFIELD. Um, forgive me, Major, but I do think it would be unfortunate if you were to go.

Pause. Trapnell waits but does not sit. The others look at Garfield.

Because, if *you'll* forgive me, gentlemen, I do think the Major has a point. And frankly, I don't think you should move next business till it's been addressed.

Pause. Trapnell sits.

You see, I wonder how often it has happened, that a group of young men, thousands of miles away from home, has had the chance to plan a new world to come home to.

Pause.

And looked at that way, I do wonder, if there's anything so bad about a politics based on the principle that if it isn't moral, then it can't be right.

Pause. The Labour group looks shifty.

TRELAWNEY. Well, I hope we'd all agree with *that*.

Slight pause.

But as to, um, the point at issue. It does strike me, there's a dramatically obvious and simple way to *test* the proposition.

They look at him.

GARFIELD. What's that?

TRELAWNEY. Well, we already have a mock parliament. We could hold a mock election.

Pause. Trapnell takes a booklet from his briefcase, and starts to look through it.

WILSON. I think you'll find, sir – it's 541a.

Trapnell reads the relevant King's Regulation. The others look on. Trapnell looks up.

GARFIELD. But, for heaven's sake, it's just pretend. I mean, to charge a soldier, under that, would be like indicting an actor who's just played Macbeth, for murder. No?

Pause.

As the Great Man said, a good army knows what it's fighting for, and loves what it knows.

Pause.

TRAPNELL. Well, I can always check. (*He puts the booklet away.*) And as you say, it would prove things, one way or the other.

Interior. Music for All: office. Late afternoon.

Garfield's office in Music for All. Trapnell is on the phone. Garfield stands.

TRAPNELL. And after all, sir, it's only simulation. I mean, to bring charges, under 541, would be like court-martialling an actor playing Bolingbroke for treason. No?

Pause.

And we must remember, as the Great Man said, a good army knows what it's fighting for and, um –

GARFIELD. Loves what it knows.

TRAPNELL. Sorry, sir. Loves what it knows.

Pause.

Well, thank you, Colonel.

Pause.

No, sir. Boling*broke*.

Exterior. Officers' garden. Early evening.

Colonel Pugh is talking to the Brigadier as they walk round the garden.

PUGH. My feeling is, you see, Brigadier, that it's really only play-acting. If you like to put it this way, if you had a chap up for pretending to be, say, Minister of Supply . . . A bit like arresting some poor thespian for – bumping off his wife, because he'd played Othello.

Pause.

And, of course, as the Great Man said, the best army is one where the troops know what they're fighting for, and love what they know.

BRIGADIER. Yes, yes.

Pause.

Which great man's that, then, Raymond?

Interior. Music for All: Pergola Cafeteria. Evening.

McRae is watching Wilson and Jacobs play chess at a table in the cafeteria. Clarke runs in.

CLARKE. (*Breathless.*) Ah. There you are.

MCRAE. Yes, what?

CLARKE. It's on.

JACOBS. What's on?

CLARKE. The mock election.

WILSON. What, King's regs notwithstanding?

CLARKE. Ar.

JACOBS. That's champion.

CLARKE. But it's got to be post-war. Like, in pretend. No service pay. No stuff about the war.

WILSON. OK.

CLARKE. And you'll have to find a Tory leader.

MCRAE. Trapnell.

CLARKE. 'Not convinced that it would be appropriate.'

WILSON. Well, then –

MCRAE. Och, no problem.

They look at Alistair McRae.

Interior: Music for All: Committee Room. Day.

The Labour group in session. Present are Atterley, Wilson, Jacobs, Simpson and Clarke. The Committee is considering a draft manifesto. Carbon copies are on the table.

We arrive during a sticky pause.

JACOBS. So, Neville, why not summarise your point?

ATTERLEY. With pleasure. (*He reads.*) 'The Labour Party stands for complete and unequivocal socialism.' Good. Agree with that. 'The attainment of this, however, cannot be achieved all at once in a democratic state', well, if you like, 'which accepts, as Labour accepts, the principle of change by peaceful evolution' – whatever that may mean – 'instead of violent revolution.' (*He looks up.*) So – that's it?

WILSON. No, it's the first of fourteen paragraphs.

ATTERLEY. I mean, that's it, in the sense of how we're planning to defend ourselves? You think, a socialist – a Labour Government – it gets itself elected, and the monopolists and Generals shut up shop, fine, lads, well played, you won, fair's fair, you carry on expropriating? What d'you want first? Have a mine, a railway, here you are?

SIMPSON. Not 'a mine', 'a railway'. Nationalisation of all transport. Of all mines.

ATTERLEY. All the loss-makers. All the basic industries that the capitalists don't want but need.

Pause.

I mean, if you want to take this – simulation, seriously.

Slight pause.

SIMPSON. He has a point.

JACOBS. Now, look. This was based up on a theory. It's there. The attainment of full socialism cannot be achieved at once. Also, it's based on what we've heard. They want full employment, National Insurance. Pensions. End to booms and slumps. They don't necessarily want – yet – the whole of British industry to be nationalised tomorrow.

ATTERLEY. Who's 'they'?

JACOBS. The blokes. The ORs. Our electors.

ATTERLEY. Oh, I see. So Labour Party socialism is, you get a lot of blokes with clipboards to go round the country asking people what they want, you add it up and that's your manifesto.

JACOBS. No –

ATTERLEY. Because, you see, it might be that you can't guarantee full employment *unless* the whole of British industry is taken over. Mm?

Interior. Music for All: Music Room. Evening.

The Election meeting. The room is a bit fuller than we've seen it before, and more excited. On the platform, the Speaker's chair and four tables, with the Election posters of the four parties pinned on the front, with the candidates – Simpson, Carter, Captain Carrington and Trelawney – sitting behind, Rubin between them. A blackboard with a list of the parties. Pressmen and press photographers present. Also, a film cameraman. In addition to the candidates and Rubin, Wilson, McRae, Atterley, Rosalind, Clarke, Jacobs, Castle, Richardson, Garfield and Trapnell, the Director of Music for All and Colonel Pugh are present.

We come into the meeting as Rubin introduces Carrington, who has been dragooned into being the Conservative candidate.

RUBIN. Good evening, friends, and welcome to the general election of the Music for All Parliament.

Applause and a little cheering.

I call upon Captain Carrington to make his statement for the Conservatives.

Carrington stands. Applause and a little booing.

CARRINGTON. Now. You know, I suspect this evening we're all going to feel is a bit like a balloon. Way above our heads, and full to bursting with hot air.

Trapnell closes his eyes.

Which is why I don't intend to rabbit on about my party's policies, but rather get off my hind legs as quick as possible and get on to the proper business of the evening.

McRae is delighted; Atterley and Simpson amused; Wilson looks blackly at McRae.

Which is to listen to *you* rabbit on about what gets *your* goat.

We see RAF Corporal Hugh Leslie – Orlando in As You Like It – *obviously annoyed that a tendency with which he has some sympathy is clearly going to be badly represented.*

And with any luck, to ferret out some answers.

Interior. Music for All: Music Room. Evening.

The speeches have been delivered: questions to Carrington have been going on some time, and they've not been sympathetic.

FIRST QUESTIONER. Mr Chairman, once again, can I ask the candidate, if the Conservative Party has a policy of security, why, in the 1930s, unemployment went beyond three millions?

CARRINGTON. Ah, yes. Well, this is it. As I have said, you will want work. That's number one. To work, and marry, raise a family. In peace, and national and international security.

Pause. He sits.

RUBIN. Um, Captain, that's your answer?

CARRINGTON. It is indeed.

RUBIN. Thank you. Well, that is the end of the time allotted for questions to the Conservative. Now, questions to the Liberal candidate.

Trelawney stands. Labour and Common Wealth hands shoot up all over the place.

Um . . . (*He spots an Indian NCO at the back.*) The um, I think, Sikh member . . .

SIKH SOLDIER. Yes. I would like to know, having heard the Liberal's speech, what difference he thinks there is between him and the representative of the socialist party.

TRELAWNEY. Well, yes. I take your point. Hearing the Labour leader's speech, one might think there was little difference.

Atterley looks pointedly at Wilson.

Though of course in practice Labour's real agenda would be clear. For we

Liberals reject both the inequalities and snobberies and vested interests of Toryism, *and* the over-regulation, queues, red tape and wastage that would inevitably result if the Labour Party came to power. (*He beams.*) So we're the best of both worlds, really.

Interior. Music for All: Music Room. Evening.

Carter is being questioned by Rosalind.

ROSALIND. Now, Mr Chairman, I may be very ignorant, so I merely ask the speaker –

ATTERLEY. (*Prompting.*) – candidate –

ROSALIND. – I see, the candidate, for information and enlightenment –

A reaction to this elaborate language.

– and if he could explain why during the anti-fascist war it was necessary to create another left-wing party?

Rosalind sits.

AUSTRALIAN HECKLER. Wasn't one enough?

Laughter. Rosalind looks at Atterley, as if to apologise for leaving herself open for the heckle. Atterley gives a reassuring gesture.

CARTER. Right. Common Wealth was born in 1941 as a movement by Sir Richard Acland –

A reaction to the 'Sir'.

Yes, that's like 'Sir Stafford Cripps', because he believed it was wrong that a whole generation had never had the chance to vote, anyone who wasn't twenty-one in 1935.

He looks around the meeting.

Further, Common Wealth opposes Labour's strategy for socialism –

'Ah!' from some Labour supporters.

– on the grounds that it is namby-pamby and half-hearted. As far as we're concerned, we're not interested in tampering with the capitalist system. We don't want a load of piecemeal, half-way house reforms. We want common ownership. Complete and unequivocal. And now.

Applause. Carter sips his water, quietly beaming to himself.

MCRAE. (*To himself.*) You bastard.

CARTER. So. Next question?

Trapnell has caught Rubin's eye.

RUBIN. Um, ah. The Honourable and Gallant –

TRAPNELL. Trapnell, AEC. I'm sad to note that once again it's a case of who can be more socialist than thou. But as that is the case, what I do think must be asked by someone, is how many wartime regulations and controls does either type of socialist intend to keep? Control of raw materials? An excess profits tax? Or any profits? State control of all investment? Rationing? And the conscription and direction of the labour force? Under the Common Wealth, will a man be told the job he has to do?

Carter plays a pantomime pause. Then he answers:

CARTER. Good question. Easy answer. Yes, yes, no, yes, until all shortages have been eliminated, no and no.

He sits to applause. Trapnell scratches his ear.

RUBIN. Well, thank you, Mr Carter. Now it's time for questions to the Labour candidate.

Trapnell sits. Carter smiles. A sea of hands. Rubin points to an insistent REME Corporal.

Yes, sir, you.

INSISTENT CORPORAL. Well, my question is quite simple. I'd like to ask *him* how he'd answer the last question to the Common Wealth.

RUBIN. Yes, Mr Simpson?

MCRAE. (*In his seat.*) Piece o' cake.

SIMPSON. Well, this is what we mean. As soon as you talk about a plan, or control or regulation, it's all vital British freedoms down the drain. Well, I don't think there's that much wrong with planning, if it's a good plan, and if you're going to stop the ramps, you need control. And of course control may mean a bit more red tape, even wastage, sometimes, but in my opinion that is nothing to the wastage of the dole queues before 1939.

A few 'Hear, hears'.

RUBIN. Next question – yes, the corporal –

Hugh Leslie stands.

LESLIE. Mr Chairman, I'd like to return to this point –

Some impatience.

Well, it's not been answered. About the direction of labour. And I liked the job I did before the war. And I'd like it back, or something like it. So it bothers me.

This has touched a chord.

WILSON. (*To himself.*) Now, careful, Simp.

SIMPSON. Well, as I said, it's not always possible to predict completely . . . It is possible, yuh, certainly, to see circumstances where direction of labour could be necessary.

A distinct feeling of unease.

After all, the unemployed didn't have much choice about the fact they didn't have a job . . .

People are not convinced; they don't want this argument dragged up again. Simpson finds a phrase among his notes, and though it's not completely relevant, it gets some sympathy back on his side.

What I'm sure about, is that the old days of using starvation to adjust exchange rates, of using human misery to rectify the currency, are gone and must not return.

Some applause. Richardson is on his feet.

RUBIN. Mr Richardson.

RICHARDSON. Look, um – my question's this. It just strikes me, that all these questions, about direction, regulation and control, they all assume that people need directing and controlling. That they won't – that they can't work out what is best themselves.

TRAPNELL. (*To himself.*) Bitter experience.

RICHARDSON. Whereas, I wonder if that's really true. I wonder, even now, even in wartime, when of course we get browned off, and flaked, and skive and scrounge . . . But at least we've got some sense, that in the army, and in the country, and the world, we do . . . rely on one another, when the chips are down. And people pour a lot of scorn on the idea that if you want to change the world you've got to change yourself . . . But I wonder, if it is that silly. Actually.

Slight pause.

I'm sorry. That didn't really come out as a question. But you take my point.

He sits down. No one feels the need to applaud.

RUBIN. (*To Simpson.*) Um – do you have an answer?

Interior. Music for All: Music Room. Evening.

The result. Reading out, Rubin. Chalking up, Wilson.

RUBIN. Ladies and gentlemen. As your returning officer, I declare the result to be as follows: The Conservatives: 17. The Liberal Party: 38. Labour: 119 –

Applause. Rubin fights over:

And Common – Common Wealth: 55.

Applause.

I declare that Labour is elected with an absolute majority. The Parliament will once again assemble at 9 p.m. on Wednesday 1st of March?

Wilson nods.

I declare the meeting closed.

Applause. As the electorate rises, and the parties assemble to celebrate or commiserate, we join Pugh and the Director.

PUGH. (*To himself.*) Damn.

DIRECTOR. I'm sorry, Colonel?

PUGH. Nothing. (*To the Director.*) Splendid show.

The Labour group on the stage congratulating Simpson.

JACOBS. Well done, Jack.

MCRAE. By the short and curlies.

WILSON. 'We shall now commence the construction of the socialist order.'

SIMPSON. Pardon?

ATTERLEY. V. I. Lenin, 1917.

Carter comes up to Richardson and Castle.

CARTER. I'm sorry.

CASTLE. Why, whatever for?

CARTER. We should have left Doug as the speaker.

Slight pause.

RICHARDSON. No.

CARTER. Oh, yes.

The socialist group has dispersed a little. Clarke has been eyeing the Common Wealth group. He turns to McRae.

CLARKE. Hey, Alistair.

MCRAE. Old pal.

CLARKE. What do you think? Of Doug?

MCRAE. Oh – I'd say – a fair to average pile of petit-bourgeois sentimental twaddle. Why?

CLARKE. Well, because, I thought – it made some sense. (*He looks at McRae.*) But obviously not.

He goes. McRae looks after him.

Interior. Brigadier's office. Day.

Brigadier and Pugh. Pugh has put a newspaper on the Brigadier's desk, folded at the result of the Election.

BRIGADIER. So. Have they got this right?

Pugh nods. Slight pause.

I see.

Pause. The Brigadier sucks his lip.

PUGH. It's a sort of – just high jinks. Snook cocking, I suppose.

BRIGADIER. I had presumed that it was educational.

PUGH. Well, yes –

BRIGADIER. Our parliamentary institutions. Oxford rules. The Speaker, Black Rod, Prayers. Do they have prayers?

PUGH. I – rather doubt it, sir.

Slight pause.

But I nonetheless do think, it's relatively –

The Brigadier stands.

BRIGADIER. Raymond, do you know about the Greeks?

Slight pause.

PUGH. The Greeks in – history?

BRIGADIER. No, the Greeks in Burg-el-Arab. You know, the ones who turn up for parade with scarlet ribbons in their hair.

Pugh looks blank.

And flashes on their uniforms. And among whom there is apparently the prospect that the officers who don't want their King back after liberation may challenge the command of those who do.

PUGH. I'd heard some gossip.

Slight pause. Pugh nods to the paper:

BRIGADIER. So – what's next?

PUGH. Uh, I think they form a cabinet. And then present a King's speech.

BRIGADIER. Do they now.

The Brigadier glares at Pugh as:

WILSON. (*Voice over.*) 'My lords and members of the House of Commons. Before us now lies one of the most difficult . . .'

Interior. Music for All: Committee Room. Evening.

Wilson, Atterley, McRae, Jacobs and Clarke meeting round a document.

JACOBS. 'Before us'?

WILSON. Mm?

JACOBS. Shouldn't it be 'before my government'?

MCRAE. Aye, right. After all, it's supposed to be the bloody king.

Simpson enters.

SIMPSON. Sorry I'm late. Something came up.

MCRAE. It's OK, Simp. We're on the speech.

WILSON. So that's – 'before my government . . .'

McRae pushes a carbon copy to Simpson.

SIMPSON. What, you've written it already?

Slight pause.

WILSON. Yes. A draft.

JACOBS. Why, is there –

SIMPSON. Well, I thought we might – before we draw up things specifically, we should discuss what happened. What went wrong.

ATTERLEY. (*With a glance at Wilson.*) What did go wrong?

SIMPSON. CW got nearly half our votes.

Pause.

WILSON. They were, it must be said, they were well organised.

JACOBS. No error.

ATTERLEY. Well, it's good to know they take things seriously.

MCRAE. But wasn't it, in fact, what Trapnell said? That they out-socialisted us?

Slight pause.

WILSON. Go on.

MCRAE. That while we were recognising that you couldn't achieve everything at once, they were demanding socialism, full and unequivocal.

ATTERLEY. That's right.

Slight pause.

SIMPSON. So what do we say now?

He's looking in the draft. Wilson has the passage.

WILSON. 'We will' – or, it'll be, our government – 'take immediate and urgent steps to place fully under state control the whole of the banking and financial machinery of the country, the transport industries, the mines.'

SIMPSON. That's it.

WILSON. That's it.

JACOBS. Well, that's OK.

MCRAE. Nothing equivocal in that.

CLARKE. Unless . . .

They look at Clarke.

MCRAE. Yuh?

CLARKE. Unless . . .

MCRAE. Go *on.*

Slight pause.

CLARKE. Well – tell me, how'd it be. The mines, and railways, like. There'd be a – Board?

WILSON. Yes, I'd imagine –

CLARKE. And trade unionists, and managers, and experts, they'd all sit on it . . .

WILSON. Well, broadly –

CLARKE. And tell the miners and footplatemen and porters what to do.

   Pause.

Because it seems to me, what people didn't like, was all the stuff about direction and control. Don't think they liked the sound of that, at all.

ATTERLEY. What, you mean they thought we were *too* left?

CLARKE. No, not too left, or right . . .

ATTERLEY. Well, it must be one or t'other, Bob –

CLARKE. It's Nobby.

ATTERLEY. Sorry?

WILSON. Name is Nobby, Neville.

ATTERLEY. Nobby. Beg your pardon.

CLARKE. 'Cos I think they think it'd be like being in the army. Actually.

   Slight pause.

And I just think, the Common Wealthers . . . I just think, the blokes felt, that they wanted them – the blokes – to end up doing back there what they done out here. That what they said, showed a bit of faith, a bit of trust, in them.

   No one responds. Clarke ups his level.

I mean, I tell you, if you want volunteers, for Ministers, I'll have the Minister of Education. 'Cos I don't want to give all children every opportunity to realise their bloody full capacity. I want to get them to fulfil capacities they never bloody realised they had.

   Pause.

ATTERLEY. Syndicalism.

CLARKE. What?

MCRAE. The idea that trade unions run individual industries, on a kind of co-operative –

CLARKE. Well, I don't know how you'd work it out. I just think that they struck a chord. That's all.

Interior. Music for All: corridor. Evening.

Jacobs, Wilson, McRae and Simpson are emerging from the Committee Room into the corridor.

JACOBS. (*To Simpson.*) So, then, what kept you?

SIMPSON. Well, it's very odd –

Interior. Music for All: Committee Room. Evening.

After the meeting. Atterley and Clarke are the last to leave.

CLARKE. Well, I'm sorry if I'm – I'm a sydalist.

ATTERLEY. Syndicalist.

CLARKE. Whatever.

ATTERLEY. No, I thought it was a good discussion. You're quite right. We need to work things out.

McRae enters.

MCRAE. Hey. Simp. Guess what.

ATTERLEY. Give up.

MCRAE. At last, life has caught up with him.

CLARKE. Life?

MCRAE. His papers.

Interior. Music for All: Committe Room. Evening.

Garfield, Simpson, McRae, Wilson, Clarke, Carter, Castle, Richardson and Trelawney. Wilson is reading a list of ministerial appointments.

WILSON. Prime Minister and Minister of Defence: A. Jacobs. Secretary of State for Foreign Affairs: N. Atterley. Chancellor of the Exchequer: A. McRae. Minister of National Insurance: me; and Minister of Education: G. E. Clarke.

TRELAWNEY. The Foreign Secretary?

Wilson looks to McRae.

MCRAE. His dress rehearsal.

CASTLE. And may we ask why Simpson's off the list?

CARTER. Been purged.

WILSON. You may indeed. Sadly, the Prime Minister as was has suffered an unexpected misfortune. His papers have caught up with him at last, and he's been posted.

General reaction.

And in fact, promoted.

MCRAE. So, hence Alf's promotion.

WILSON. And the fact we've no one at the Board of Trade.

GARFIELD. (*To Simpson.*) Congratulations.

SIMPSON. Thanks.

Wilson hands out papers.

WILSON. Now, we have copies of the King's Speech. I'm sorry, they're somewhat creased and amended, but I think they're readable, and we are looking forward to amendments from the Opposition.

CASTLE. Yes, well, we want to bring that up. As you know, Common Wealth is extremely unhappy at being cast in the role of Opposition in the conventional sense. But we are of course prepared to amend bills when they offer undue compensation to big business, or –

MCRAE. Or omit to emphasise the spiritual dimension.

CASTLE. However, we would obviously be happier with amendments forthcoming from the real Opposition parties.

Everyone looks at Trelawney.

TRELAWNEY. Yes. The Anti-Statists. Where is Captain Carrington?

WILSON. I think – it's fair to say – that Captain Carrington has decided to retire from public life.

MCRAE. So if anybody's got a lot of Tory friends – like Corporal Richardson –

CARTER. Look, this constant sniping is beginning to –

GARFIELD. Yes. Please. Please, gentlemen. Can we try to –

CARTER. Bloody turn it up.

Interior. Music for All: dressing room. Afternoon.

The dressing rooms for As You Like It *are quite makeshift, separated by blankets, behind the stage of the Music Room. Leslie is in the costume and half-way through the make-up of Orlando. He is surrounded by Carter, Castle and Richardson.*

LESLIE. You see, I'm not, in fact . . . I only asked a question.

Pause.

I mean, I quite enjoy it, public speaking, I was in a parliament, mock parliament, at school. I was the Social Credit candidate. I mean, I quite enjoy it all.

The Common Wealthers are breathing deeply.

Now, look. All right. I'll do it. But I won't promise an amendment every session. But I'll speak, and try and make the thing – feel real.

Great relief.

CARTER. Well done. Good man.

CASTLE. We'll help in every way, of course.

RICHARDSON. With typing.

CARTER. Drafting. Meetings. Caucuses.

CASTLE. You've done the right thing.

RICHARDSON. Hugh.

CASTLE. We're really very grateful.

Rosalind, costumed, pops her head round the corner of the blanket.

ROSALIND. They've called five minutes, Hugh.

LESLIE. All right.

Rosalind goes. The Common Wealthers turn to leave.

You see – I must repeat it, make it absolutely clear. I'm not paid up or anything. I mean, you could say, that I'm not really a Conservative at all.

The three turn back.

CARTER. (*Conspiratorially to Leslie.*) No One Need Ever Know.

Slight pause. The Common Wealthers go. A pause. Rosalind puts her head back round the blankets.

ROSALIND. (*As a cod gangster.*) So who's the heavy mob?

LESLIE. So who's the leader of the Tory Party?

ROSALIND. Winston Churchill.

LESLIE. Me.

Interior. Music for All: corridor. Evening.

McRae and Richardson are at the door, outside the Music Room. McRae is giving out cards, on which Richardson writes down names of constituencies, noting them down on a list as he does so. A Geordie ATS is coming in.

MCRAE. Good evening, miss, which party d'you support?

GEORDIE. Oh, I suppose, I'm a Liberal.

MCRAE. And where d'you come from?

GEORDIE. Newcastle.

MCRAE. (*Checking his list.*) Another bloody Geordie, eh?

RICHARDSON. South's free.

GEORDIE. Well, no, in fact –

MCRAE. Then south it is.

   Richardson hands her a card. The next arrival is a Lancastrian Sergeant.

MCRAE. Now, pal. And what's your party?

LANCASTRIAN. Well –

MCRAE. Say Labour. Where d'you come from?

LANCASTRIAN. Uh –

MCRAE. Say, Burnley?

   Richardson shakes his head.

Oh, I'm sorry, pal. Full up. D'you fancy Macclesfield?

Interior. Music for All: Music Room. Evening.

*The hall is fuller than it was for the election. It is now set up as in
Parliament, with chairs facing each other, and a 'despatch box' in the centre
aisle. There is also an area at the back marked 'Visitors' Gallery'. Rubin is in
the chair; Wilson as Clerk; McRae, Atterley, Clarke and Jacobs as the
'Government'; Castle, Carter and Richardson; Trelawney; Garfield, Leslie
and Trapnell. Jacobs stands to begin the King's speech. There are cheers.*

RUBIN. Order, order. Although strictly the business of another place, I call
upon the Prime Minister – the new Prime Minister – to read the King's
Speech to the House.

   More cheers. Jacobs begins:

JACOBS. My lords and members of the House of Commons: Before my
Government and before all my subjects lies one of the most difficult,
perhaps *the* most difficult as well as the most momentous periods in our
history. We have emerged victorious from the greatest war in human

history, to find ourselves faced with tasks of truly no less magnitude than that of winning the war itself.

Interior. Music for All: corridor. Evening.

Seeing no one else approaching, Richardson slips into the Music Room to hear the King's Speech. We hear, but do not see, Jacobs.

JACOBS. In this gigantic task, the transition from a wartime to a peace economy is naturally our first concern.

Interior. Music for All: Music Room. Evening.

Jacobs is continuing his speech, with Richardson listening.

JACOBS. My government will take immediate and urgent steps to place fully under – public ownership the whole of the banking and financial machinery of the country, the transport and the fuel industries.

This bit is new:

In the organisation of these public industries, the government will seek to build upon those forms of self-administration and co-operative endeavour – the Joint Production Committees and the like – that have marked the dramatic effort of the war years.

Richardson hears a tap on the glass window in the door, turns and sees another Member has arrived. He goes out into the corridor.

In the conviction that our people have now demonstrated to themselves and to the world capacities they never dreamt that they possessed.

Interior. Music for All: corridor. Evening.

Rosalind has arrived at the desk.

RICHARDSON. Well, strictly, you need a constituency. Where do you come from?

ROSALIND. What, originally?

RICHARDSON. Well, in civvy street. Before the war.

ROSALIND. Jerusalem.

She goes in, past Richardson. Meanwhile, we might have heard Jacobs:

JACOBS. (*Out of vision.*) And it is with this positive commitment to the strengths of all our people that we place before the House those further measures, in both foreign and domestic policy, that are in our view vital for the economic welfare of our countrymen, and the future of our continent and world.

Interior. Music for All: Music Room. Evening.

Jacobs is concluding.

JACOBS. Our tasks are many and are grievous. But we are a great and tenacious nation, and given that same spirit of unity and determination which animated us during the dark days of 1940, even as we won the war against almost overwhelming odds, so we shall now achieve the winning of the peace.

He sits. Applause. Rosalind is at the back of the hall, peering down towards the front, looking for McRae, Atterley and Wilson.

RUBIN. The Honourable Member for Cardigan.

Carter stands. Rosalind spots the trio and comes down.

CARTER. Mr Speaker. We welcome the vast majority of the provisions outlined in the gracious speech, but have moved the amendment on the order paper because –

As Carter continues, Rosalind whispers to McRae, Atterley and Wilson. There is a lot of shaking of heads and alarm.

– of our regret that the Government has not acknowledged the necessity for a democratic federation of European countries –

The whisperers conclude, McRae goes and whispers to Clarke.

– to avoid the perpetuation of the national scramble for markets –

McRae whispers to Clarke. Atterley and Rosalind hurry out. Wilson glances at his watch and bites his lip.

– that certainly led to one world war, and arguably contributed to the second. I beg to move.

He sits.

RUBIN. The Honourable Member for Northampton.

Leslie stands.

LESLIE. Mr Speaker. I have to tell you that the Conservative Party does not welcome the provisions outlined in the, uh – the gracious speech.

Interior. Music for All: corridor. Evening.

Wilson, McRae and Clarke are hurrying along the corridor towards the lobby.

WILSON. Now, Nobby, can you get a truck? Your jeep, or something?

CLARKE. Uh – not now. Not at night.

They have reached the lobby.

Interior. Music for All: lobby. Evening.

McRae, Clarke and Wilson enter the lobby.

MCRAE. Well, I see no alternative.

Wilson looks at McRae, who taps the side of his nose.

Interior. GHQ Public Relations: corridor. Evening.

McRae is passing bicycles out of the Cuttings Room to Wilson and Clarke. The last bicycle.

MCRAE. Right, then. Let's go.

They hurry out, with their bicycles – Clarke carrying two, as McRae locks the Cuttings Room door, and follows his comrades.

Interior. Charlotte's apartment. Evening.

Charlotte opens the door, to see McRae, Wilson and Clarke with their bicycles.

CHARLOTTE. Thank God you're here.

WILSON. We couldn't get a truck.

CHARLOTTE. The bikes are perfect.

WILSON. We're one short.

CHARLOTTE. No problem.

Charlotte's own bicycle is near the door. She ushers them in. Atterley is shovelling books, pamphlets and newspapers into sacks. Clarke, McRae and Wilson go to help. During the following, a piece of paper will fall from Wilson's pocket on to the floor, unnoticed in the general hurry.

MCRAE. So how d'you hear?

Charlotte is taking torches from a cupboard.

CHARLOTTE. My maid has a boyfriend in the Chief of Police's secretariat.

WILSON. Why now?

Charlotte doesn't so much ignore the question, as remember something more immediately pressing. Hurrying into another room:

CHARLOTTE. The rope. I mustn't let you go without the rope.

ATTERLEY. EAM/ELAS have declared themselves the government of the liberated territories.

He goes out after Charlotte.

CLARKE. (*To McRae.*) EAM/E – what?

MCRAE. Greek partisans.

WILSON. And in Egypt there are several thousand –

Charlotte appears with rope.

CHARLOTTE. Right. Here's rope.

Atterley appears with a metal tray.

ATTERLEY. The tray.

Most people look at him blankly.

Let's go.

Interior. Officers' Mess: bar. Night.

Trapnell is enjoying a large whisky. Colonel Pugh approaches.

PUGH. Well, evening, John.

Trapnell makes to stand.

TRAPNELL. Hallo, sir.

Pugh waves Trapnell not to get up, and sits himself.

PUGH. Good night?

TRAPNELL. Oh, MFA.

PUGH. The Soviet.

TRAPNELL. First Wednesday of the month.

PUGH. Still formulating blueprints for the workers' paradise.

TRAPNELL. I s'pose, to be expected.

PUGH. Well, that's certainly the view of Dr Goebbels.

Pause.

TRAPNELL. Sorry?

PUGH. As expressed on German radio. (*With a slight, humourless smile.*)
One hell of a stink, John.

Pugh moves away.

Exterior. Road near camp. Night.

*In a little siding, Wilson waits, with his bicycle and haversack of literature.
McRae and Clarke arrive, also loaded.*

MCRAE. Beg pardon. Puncture.

WILSON. Glory be. Unload.

He picks up a haversack and goes off, leaving the other two to unload.

Exterior. ATS camp. Night.

Atterley has arrived here with his bicycle a few moments ago. He has dug a shallow trench beneath – or cut a small hole in – the wire fence round the ATS camp. Between the fence and the nearest hut is an exposed, lit area. Atterley has fixed up a makeshift pulley arrangement, by which the metal tray – loaded with literature – can be pulled over to the nearest hut, unloaded and pulled back. Wilson arrives with his load.

WILSON. Neville.

ATTERLEY. What kept you?

Atterley already taking the literature and piling it on the tray.

WILSON. Guess who had a puncture.

Exterior. ATS hut. Night.

The nearest ATS hut is on stilts. Rosalind waits there, with the other end of the rope. She feels a tug on the rope. She starts to pull. We see the tray and the literature sliding across towards her.

Exterior. ATS camp. Night.

Wilson watches Atterley playing out the rope that will pull the tray back.

WILSON. Well I never.

ATTERLEY. Infinite resourcefulness. Next load.

Exterior. ATS hut. Night.

Rosalind has unloaded the literature and towed it under the hut. She tugs on the rope and the empty tray slides away from her.

Exterior. ATS camp. Night.

Clarke and Wilson arrive with two haversacks.

ATTERLEY. How many more?

WILSON. That's it.

ATTERLEY. Right. Nobby. Scram.

Clarke scurries away as Wilson helps Atterley load the literature on the tray.

Interior. Charlotte's apartment. Night.

Charlotte stands in her main room. Two Egyptian Policemen enter from another room.

CHARLOTTE. Now, you are satisfied?

FIRST POLICEMAN. Oh, yes. For the moment, we are satisfied.

The second Policeman notices something on the floor. He nods to the first Policeman, who picks it up. It's the paper Wilson dropped. The two Policemen look at it. On one side is a document headed 'Middle East GHQ – Most Secret'. The Policeman looks at Charlotte, who smiles. The Policeman turns it over. On the other side of the paper is a list of notes for the Clerk, on the order of events of the King's Speech meeting.

FIRST POLICEMAN. And what is this, please?

Charlotte takes the paper.

CHARLOTTE. I have a friend – a British officer. Apparently, the troops have set up this – a legislature. My friend goes to their meetings, sees they don't get out of hand. Apparently, all fun and games.

Pause.

FIRST POLICEMAN. Yes, so they say.

Slight pause.

CHARLOTTE. So who says?

FIRST POLICEMAN. That I cannot say.

Slight pause.

CHARLOTTE. Why not?

FIRST POLICEMAN. I am a loyal servant of the state. I therefore cannot hear the things they broadcast on the German radio.

Charlotte looks confused.

Exterior. Pyramids. Dawn.

McRae, Wilson and Clarke, with their bicycles, watching the dawn.

MCRAE. Well, you saw a kind of action, Nobby.

CLARKE. Mm.

McRae wanders a little apart.

I don't get all this Greek stuff.

WILSON. Well, it's the usual division. There's a camp at Burg-el-Arab. And the officers have them on parade, in the midday sun, and scream at them about how they're going to get the King back and all the Communists'll be exterminated.

Slight pause.

CLARKE. But why are they raiding flats?

Pause. Wilson decides to explain.

WILSON. Well, notionally, it's the local cops combating Communist subversion. In fact, of course, it's our brass, who know things are brewing. And they think that if there is some form of – mutiny, then the progressive Greeks will need help. And will get it.

Pause.

CLARKE. Uh, that's – serious.

WILSON. We're serious.

CLARKE. Well, sure. I meant, like, uh, for real.

WILSON. So you don't think that the other stuff's for real? The parliament, and so on?

Clarke says nothing.

Because for me that's absolutely serious.

Slight pause.

(*Lighter.*) So do you have news of your brother?

CLARKE. Well, he's in a camp. 'Somewhere in occupied . . .' But still alive.

Wilson smiles, then looks at Clarke.

WILSON. Do you know the story of the Model Army?

Clarke shakes his head.

Cromwell's new Model Army, in the English Civil War. The troops were largely volunteers, the new masterless men, from the towns and forests, who had been brought up during the most terrible depression, in the 1630s, anybody could remember. And they saw themselvess, not as cannon fodder, but as citizens in uniform. And they knew that they were needed by the Parliamentary Forces, to win the war, and they were determined, when it was all over, that they weren't just shrugged off and sent home. And they elected representatives, called 'agitators', who drew up plans, for the England that would come to pass, with universal suffrage, annual parliaments, no forced conscription, and the common ownership of land. And they said, that's what we're fighting for. And Cromwell said, well, that's OK by me.

Pause.

But the point is, that it wasn't, really. And when the main fighting finished, Cromwell wanted to disband the army, those he didn't need to send to Ireland, to put down rebellion there. But the troops refused. They were owed back-pay. They went to Newmarket, and they resolved not to disband until their grievances were met. And they elected, from below, a council of the agitators, which would run the army in the interests of the common people. And even further, they insisted Cromwell meet with them, and discuss their plan, which was called 'The Agreement of the People'. And they met in Putney, for ten days, in October and November 1647, and they debated the creation of a new heaven and a new earth in the country they'd just won. A New – Jerusalem.

Pause. Wilson looks at Clarke and smiles. McRae is coming back to Clarke and Wilson.

CLARKE. So then, what happened?

McRae arrives.

MCRAE. Well, I canna speak for you folk, but this morning freshness, vaporous and inexpressible, is sure as hell intoxicating me.

Interior. GHQ Public Relations: corridor. Morning.

McRae is carrying two bicycle along the corridor, with an extremely irritated Ballantine carrying a third.

BALLANTINE. I mean, for heaven's sake, mate.

MCRAE. (*Clenched teeth.*) Bill, this thing was an emergency.

BALLANTINE. We are dealing here with highly sensitive and delicate machines . . .

MCRAE. Aye, I know that.

BALLANTINE. Not a pile of pushbikes for your chums to borrow for a joyride –

Outside the office door, he puts down the two bicycles.

MCRAE. Bill. This thing was not a joyride.

CARRINGTON. (*Out of vision.*) Sergeant!

McRae, with a look at Ballantine, goes into the office.

Interior. GHQ Public Relations: office. Morning.

McRae enters to Carrington. We can see the still furious Ballantine picking up a second bicycle to take it to the cuttings room.

MCRAE. Sir.

CARRINGTON. Sergeant, not only are you late –

MCRAE. I'm sorry, sir, I –

CARRINGTON. But there has been some bint on the phone since dawn –

MCRAE. Some bint?

Ballantine, through the doorway, as he picks up the third bike:

BALLANTINE. And you're still one short.

MCRAE. I know.

CARRINGTON. Apparently, your racket's been on German radio.

MCRAE. (*Following him.*) My racket? What? What racket?

Interior. GHQ Public Relations: corridor. Morning.

McRae follows Carrington out of the office; Ballantine outside the cuttings room tending to a bicycle.

CARRINGTON. You know. Your parliament. The thing you roped me into.

He leaves.

MCRAE. (*With a look to Ballantine.*) German radio.

Interior. Brigadier's office. Day.

An officers' meeting. Those present include the Brigadier, Pugh, the Signals Colonel, the Other Colonel and a General. It is clear it is the Brigadier's meeting, and the General is a little distanced. The Signals Colonel is reading from a transcript:

SIGNALS COLONEL. 'We have received reports that British soldiers serving in Cairo have formed their own Parliament. At recent "elections" the Labour Party won with a staggering majority.' That's the German European Service. English. And this is the German Home Service: 'In domestic politics also, Churchill's position has been shaken. In Cairo, British soldiers have set up a Parliament for which they have held an election. The result is most interesting. The Conservative received 17 votes, the Liberals 18, and the Labour Party, together with a communist wing, 174. This is of course how things started over here in the critical phase of the First World War. Over here, things began with the Workers' and Soldiers' Councils.' And then he goes on to the usual stuff about the Jewish war, and British plutocrats, and Bolshevik conspiracies, and so on.

Pause.

PUGH. In fact, they've got it wrong. The Liberals got 38.

Pause.

GENERAL. What is this communist wing they talk about?

PUGH. That's Common Wealth, sir. You know, the ones who won the Skipton by-election.

Slight pause.

They'll be delighted. Labour calls them soft.

BRIGADIER. I should report that I've received an intimation from the W.O. that they are pretty browned off with this thing.

OTHER COLONEL. Surprise, surprise.

BRIGADIER. So – comments?

OTHER COLONEL. (*Taking the transcript.*) Workers' and Soldiers' Councils. German Soviets. Could have mentioned the same thing in the Russian Army two years earlier.

PUGH. Um, Brigadier, I'm not sure the analogy –

OTHER COLONEL. Or indeed some armies not a million miles from here.

Pause. Everyone looks at the Other Colonel.

SIGNALS OFFICER. What do you mean, Colonel?

OTHER COLONEL. Well, you take your pick. The Yugoslavs, the Eyeties . . .

GENERAL. And of course the Greeks.

OTHER COLONEL. Indeed.

Everyone turns to the General.

GENERAL. It might be worth remembering, that in the Greek Army, and the navy for that matter, we have a force riven from top to bottom and by all accounts set fair to mutiny.

Expressions of surprise and shock from the Colonels.

Yesterday, a group of thirteen left-wing officers presented the Greek Premier in exile, that's Mr Tsouderos, with demands for a post-liberation Government of National Unity. On his orders, six of those thirteen officers have been arrested. It is our opinion that there is a possibility – or indeed a likelihood – that the radicals will attempt to relieve the royalist commanders of the First Brigade at Burg-el-Arab, and indeed, of sectors of the Greek Navy at Alex.

Slight pause.

An adventure which we'd almost certainly be called upon to deal with. And which would no doubt be aided and abetted by our very own and home-grown revolutionary cadres here.

OTHER COLONEL. Pugh's awkward squad.

GENERAL. Exactly. It is frightening to speculate, what might occur, if we were forced – as well we might be – to institute some form of military blockade. What the 'comrades' might feel themselves compelled to do.

Pause.

PUGH. Look.

Slight pause.

Look. I could prepare, if it's agreed, I could prepare suggestions for some changes – in procedures for the Parliament, which would . . .

OTHER COLONEL. I'd have thought it's very easy, Raymond. (*Tossing the transcript on the table.*) 'Take away this bauble.'

Interior. Room. Day.

We see the present-day Steve Wilson, being interviewed, in close-up.

WILSON. No, there's no doubt the election was the crucial thing. Because it showed the strength of feeling. Because it showed it wasn't just a game. And the reason why we didn't spot the danger was precisely that it was so heady and euphoric. It was a honeymoon, and like a honeymoon, of course, it couldn't last.

Closing titles of Episode Two.

Episode Three

Interior. Signals Colonel's office. Morning.

Jacobs has just entered the office of his colonel.

SIGNALS COLONEL. Ah, come in, Jacobs. Do sit down.

Jacobs sits.

Have a gasper?

JACOBS. Thank you, sir.

Jacobs takes a cigarette.

SIGNALS COLONEL. I hear glowing reports of your sterling efforts on the Treasury bench.

JACOBS. (*After a second.*) Well, thank you, sir.

SIGNALS COLONEL. A foretaste, things to come?

JACOBS. We hope so, sir.

SIGNALS COLONEL. Indeed. Now what you're in here for, is the matter of your application for a posting.

Pause.

JACOBS. Yes, sir?

SIGNALS COLONEL. Now you applied, I think I'm right, to be transferred to AMGOT. Civil admin. of the occupied territories. Thought that your experience, your union work would come in handy.

JACOBS. Yes, sir – ?

SIGNALS COLONEL. Well, it's come through. You're off to Naples. Get the Eyeties sorted out.

Pause.

Well done.

JACOBS. Sir, I made my application seven months ago.

SIGNALS COLONEL. Red tape. (*He puts out his hand.*) Congratulations, Jacobs. Desolate to lose you, but I know you want to go.

Jacobs still doesn't know quite how to react, but he shakes his Colonel's hand.

A new age, Jacobs. Clear away the rubble and the desolation. Build a new world, new foundations, grand and fine.

He looks at Jacobs.

I'm envious.

Interior. Music for All: Music Room. Evening.

The end of the performance of As You Like It. *During it, Atterley rushes out and:*

DUKE SENIOR. Proceed, proceed. We will begin these rites,
As we do trust they'll end, in true delights.

Applause, the beginning of the call. Rosalind and Leslie as Orlando come down to take the first call. After her bow, Rosalind rushes off, somewhat to Leslie's surprise.

Interior. Music for All: dressing rooms. Evening.

Atterley is in his dressing room, ripping off his costume. He hears Rosalind rush past into the next dressing-room area.

Interior. Music for All: dressing rooms. Evening.

Rosalind rushes into her dressing room, and begins to change.

Interior. Music for All: dressing-room corridor. Evening.

Atterley, still half-made-up, but changed, waits for Rosalind. She appears, changed but still made-up also. They rush off together, passing Leslie, still costumed as Orlando, who enters from the curtain call, and looks after them.

Interior. Music for All: lobby. Evening.

The As You Like It *audience is beginning to leave the building. Atterley and Rosalind rush past and through them to the exit.*

Interior. Bookshop: basement. Night.

In the bookshop basement are a number of people – mostly but not all in various uniforms – including Charlotte and Wilson.

WILSON. The thing is, nothing's planned. This all blew up so quickly.

Someone looks quizzically at Wilson, as if to say 'that's life'. There is a low knock at the back door. Charlotte goes to answer it. A moment. Then she admits the still half-made-up Atterley and Rosalind.

ROSALIND. What country, friends, is this?

CHARLOTTE. Who cares. Come in.

Rosalind and Atterley join Wilson and others poring over a map on the table.

WILSON. Now look. If we could get supplies to somewhere here, we could get it on to a felucca . . .

ROSALIND. Whose felucca?

Interior. Heliopolis RAF camp: hangar. Morning.

Clarke and Beatty enter the hangar – in which parts of various damaged aircraft are arranged in order to be reassembled – and walk down it together towards the engine sector where they work. Beatty is lecturing his friend, who chooses to aquiesce with a smile and occasional nod.

BEATTY. Right. So we'll meet up at the Victory Club. And then we'll proceed in a broad sweep down the Kasr to the flicks. And we will be summoned urgently to no emergency committee meetings, and we will not suddenly require use of Flight's jeep, and my bint who is called June will not be lectured on the need for the immediate expropriation of the moneyed classes in the interests of the international –

Clarke, still smiling, is preparing himself for work. Beatty has noticed a note fixed to the engine casing.

Hey. Hey, Mata Hari.

Clarke turns and looks, puzzled.

CLARKE. Pardon?

Beatty gestures to a note that he has left on the seat.

BEATTY. (*Mock conspiratorial.*) 'Note.'

Exterior. City of the Dead. Late afternoon.

The cemetery outside Cairo. Clarke arrives in his jeep. Men – including one Egyptian Arab – begin to transfer packages of food from the jeep on to the backs of donkeys. There is at least one lookout.

Exterior. Banks of river. Early evening.

The donkeys arrive at the banks of a river, where a felucca awaits them, and a couple of other people, including Steve Wilson. The packages begin to be unloaded from the donkeys on to the felucca.

Interior. Cinema foyer. Evening.

Beatty, his WAAF Girlfriend June, and Clarke hurry into a cinema foyer. They're late. To the ticket booth.

BEATTY. I mean, for Christ's sake, Nobby. Just this once. Three please.

He buys tickets.

CLARKE. I'm sorry, Bill.

BEATTY. 'Ooh, I'm so sorry, had to run this little errand.' Like, for the hundredth time.

CLARKE. I said I'm sorry, Bill.

They are hurrying towards the cinema.

BEATTY. I mean, the British Army, High Command, war on all fronts, global conflagration, is really going to take the bother to close down your effing talking-shop?

Of course, that's not been what Clarke's been up to. He looks puzzled, which June misinterprets as him looking chastened. She looks considerately at her date's best friend.

Interior. Cinema auditorium. Evening.

Clarke, Beatty and June are moving along a fullish row to find their seats. The Pathe news is in full cry: news from the Eastern Front. Continuing victories in the Balkans are announced: there are cheers. Then, suddenly, the film grinds down. We hear that groan of discontent that accompanies failed film. Clarke, Beatty and June stop in their tracks. Suddenly, from above, there are spotlights and voices, and leaflets are flung from the projection room, fluttering down through the smoke over the audience:

VOICES. Greek mutiny! The heroic Greeks blockaded at Burg-el-Arab! Support the anti-fascist freedom fighters! Support the struggle for a Free Greece! And –

> *Suddenly, we hear the crash of a closing window. We see a couple of off-duty MPs hurry out of the cinema, and the film begins again, a moment or two after it left off.*

BEATTY. (*Looking at the leaflet.*) This is the effing limit, Nob.

Interior. Cinema foyer. Evening.

The MPs come out of the cinema. Atterley is there, in the foyer. The MPs pass him. He breathes deeply.

Interior. Bar. Evening.

Wilson sits at a table with three beers. McRae and Atterley hurry in, breathless, and sit down with Wilson. They raise their glasses to each other in a toast. The door of the bar opens, and two MPs enter. They look around for a moment. They go out.

WILSON. You did it?

MCRAE. Yup. How did the food stuff go?

WILSON. Oh, fine. Full marks to Nobby.

MCRAE. Right.

> *They sup their beer.*

Now all we've go to cope with is, that on Wednesday we are minus one Prime Minister.

WILSON. I'm sorry?

MCRAE. Alf's got his posting. AMGOT.

WILSON. Good for him. So, who on earth –

ATTERLEY. Well, I would have thought it's obvious.

> *They look at him.*

Unrealised capacities. The need to show a bit of bloody trust in. Actually.

Interior. Brigadier's office. Evening.

The Brigadier, Pugh, Trapnell, Garfield, the Director of Music For All. They have drinks. Garfield and the Director have just read a document.

DIRECTOR. You're going to read this out tomorrow, Brigadier?

BRIGADIER. It's going to be read out, yes, certainly.

Pause.

GARFIELD. You didn't think sir, that it might have been – appropriate – to have some kind of consultation with the Parliament's Committee?

BRIGADIER. I certainly considered it, yes, Dr Garfield. (*Waving the decanter.*) Top up?

Garfield puts his hand over his glass.

Um – ?

DIRECTOR. No thank you, Brigadier.

GARFIELD. (*Outburst.*) I must say, that I don't think it'll go down well, I must report that to you.

BRIGADIER. Oh, well. 'Into each life.'

GARFIELD. It's far too late to cancel it, you know. It's publicised all over Cairo.

BRIGADIER. Yes. We're aware of that, unfortunately.

DIRECTOR. So do you not think, Brigadier –

PUGH. In fact, we wondered, under those – these circumstances, if Dr Garfield, if you'd be prepared to communicate the contents of this document.

GARFIELD. You mean, to the Committee?

BRIGADIER. No.

GARFIELD. To the meeting as a whole?

PUGH. That's right.

GARFIELD. Colonel, you must be – No, I'm sorry, gentlemen. It's a military matter. Not for me.

BRIGADIER. Well, yes. I understand.

Pause. Suddenly:

Splendid to see you both.

DIRECTOR. We meet at Philippi.

Slight pause.

GARFIELD. Brigadier, would you like me to keep this copy of your document?

BRIGADIER. No, I don't think so, Dr Garfield.

Garfield puts the copy on the desk.

GARFIELD. Good evening, Brigadier.

Garfield and the Director go out. Pause.

PUGH. (*To Trapnell.*) I'm sorry, John.

Interior. Music for All: lobby. Evening.

Geoffrey Carter is entering the Music for All building from the street. He shows his season ticket, and is continuing on in when he hears an exchange between the Admissions Clerk and an American journalist.

AMERICAN JOURNALIST. I'm press, sweetheart.

ADMISSIONS CLERK. Oh, I'm sorry, sir. No press or civilians this evening.

AMERICAN JOURNALIST. What, is this serious?

Carter sees two Military Police entering the lobby. Wilson appears, in a hurry.

CARTER. Steve, what the hell is –

WILSON. Geoff. Quick. Come with me.

Interior. Music for All: dressing rooms. Evening.

The dressing rooms behind the stage of the Music Room. Still a certain amount of As You Like It *detritus remaining. The growing sound of people entering the Music Room beyond. We follow Wilson and Carter in. Garfield is speaking, to Clarke, Richardson, Atterley, McRae and Rubin.*

GARFIELD. So, I must report, although I was instructed not to consult with, or even inform your committee – it's obvious enough what's going on.

Pause.

I was telephoned this morning and instructed to exclude press and civilians.

Pause.

WILSON. So, what's going to happen?

GARFIELD. A statement will be made by Major Trapnell.

RICHARDSON. Closing the Parliament?

Pause.

GARFIELD. No, not quite.

Pause.

Look I'm in a most invidious position. Really. I am sorry.

He makes to go.

MCRAE. Will they be here? The Brig and Co.?

GARFIELD. I think you can assume they will.

ATTERLEY. MPs?

CARTER. They're here already.

RICHARDSON. Bloody hell.

Pause. Garfield goes out. Pause. A sense of frustration, of not knowing quite what ball-game they're now in.

WILSON. Comrades. The question seems quite simple. If we're ordered to stop this evening's session, what do we do? Do we accept the order, shut up shop, or do we carry on?

Variously:

CARTER. Oh, come on, Steve, of course you carry on.

MCRAE. We can't just cave in.

RICHARDSON. It's all been advertised, there'll be hundreds in there –

ATTERLEY. Are already.

RUBIN. Gentlemen. May I say a word?

Silence.

Gentlemen. I agreed to be the Speaker of your Parliament because of my general interest in the rules of constitutional procedure. I have deliberately kept myself apart from the political purposes of the Parliament, because that does not concern me, and as an officer from another country, I felt it was not appropriate for me to intervene.

Pause.

On the other hand, I have of course been noticing what's going on. It is clear that what is happening here is not merely an exercise, neither a lesson in parliamentary procedure to increase the general knowledge of the troops, nor simply a platform for the discussion of the issues of the day. It is clear it is much more than that.

Pause.

I think in fact it is one of the most exciting and creative undertakings I have been involved with for a long time. I shall accordingly do everything in my power to ensure that this evening's session goes ahead to its conclusion, peacefully. If the military authorities decide to use MPs to close the meeting, then, of course, it's up to you.

Reaction: relief, smiles.

WILSON. Well. Well, thank you very much indeed, Lieutenant.

Rubin makes to go. Then turns back to McRae:

RUBIN. 'I spy strangers.'

MCRAE. Eh?

RUBIN. A traditional parliamentary cry.

He winks at McRae and goes out. Pause.

RICHARDSON. So what does happen if they use MPs?

ATTERLEY. Well surely, that's an academic question.

CARTER. Why?

ATTERLEY. Because there'll be the best part of four hundred people out there, and I frankly doubt if anything decided here and now would make a fig of difference to what they do. So, shall we go?

The group makes to go.

MCRAE. Hey. Alf.

ATTERLEY. What?

WILSON. Right. Alf's been posted.

CARTER. When?

WILSON. And we're short of one Prime Minister.

Slight pause.

MCRAE. So. Nominations?

WILSON. You.

MCRAE. I'm the Chancellor of the Exchequer. It's my Bill.

WILSON. If we get that far.

CARTER. Then Steve.

WILSON. Oh, no.

CARTER. Why not?

WILSON. Because . . .

Slight pause.

Not four hundred people, Geoffrey. Sorry. Everybody has his limits. Those are mine.

ATTERLEY. Propose the Minister of Education.

RICHARDSON. Seconded.

MCRAE. All those in favour.

Everyone except the Minister of Education in favour, briskly.

WILSON. Excellent. Let's go.

And they do. Clarke is banjaxed.

CLARKE. (*At the departing backs.*) Eh, Neville . . . Look, for Christ's sake – Alistair . . .

McRae turns back to Clarke.

MCRAE. Hey, Nob. Capacities you never thought you had.

Interior. Music for All: corridor. Evening.

Trelawney is on door duty tonight, with the list, giving constituency cards to people. There is quite a queue. Carter appears, and hangs about.

TRELAWNEY. (*To a New Zealand airman.*) Right. If you must. North Christchurch. Front on the left.

The next is a Padre, of the rank of Major.

Good evening, sir. And where d'you hail from?

PADRE. Oh, um – Oswestry.

TRELAWNEY. (*Writing on a card.*) And your party, may I ask?

PADRE. Crossbench?

He takes the card quickly and goes in.

CARTER. (*Quickly.*) Frank . . .

Interior. Music for All: Music Room. Evening.

The hall is filling up nicely. We pan round, past the Visitors' Gallery, to Wilson and Richardson, with Leslie:

WILSON. So I'd advise you seriously to think about what you might say, if we actually get to make a statement.

LESLIE. Oh, Jesus. Jesus *Christ*.

He flails off. Wilson and Richardson are surprised by Leslie's vehemence.

Interior. Music for All: corridor. Evening.

Trelawney is on the door, Carter is still there. They see the Brigadier, Colonel Pugh and an unhappy-looking Trapnell, coming past.

BRIGADIER. Good evening, Lieutenant.

TRELAWNEY. Evening . . .

The entourage enters the Music Room.

. . . Brigadier.

Interior. Music Room. Evening.

Wilson is being collared by the Padre.

PADRE. Excuse me, Warrant Officer.

WILSON. Yes, sir?

PADRE. Are you in charge?

WILSON. Well – what is it about, sir?

Wilson aware that Pugh and the Brigadier are seating themselves in the Visitors' Gallery.

PADRE. I have been instructed to take prayers, before the meeting.

WILSON. Prayers?

PADRE. Yes. Parliamentary prayers.

WILSON. Well, we don't – we haven't usually . . .

PADRE. I am told the Brigadier is most insistent.

Slight pause.

WILSON. Well, then. Fine. I'll tell the Speaker.

PADRE. Thank you.

The Padre withdraws. Clarke, who has been floating on the edge of this conversation, grabs Wilson.

CLARKE. Cromwell.

WILSON. (*Making to hurry away.*) Now don't you worry, Nobby –

CLARKE. Cromwell.

Wilson turns to Clarke.

WILSON. Cromwell?

CLARKE. The Model Army. And how they drew up plans. And debated them with Cromwell. Well, I asked you then, I ask you now. What happened then?

Slight pause.

WILSON. Um – look –

Slight pause.

Look. I've got to collar Rubin, Nobby.

Wilson hurries away. Clarke looks about. MPs are standing round. Clarke goes out into the corridor.

Interior. Music for All: corridor. Evening.

Trelawney has just admitted Beatty and June.

TRELAWNEY. OK, now, at the front and on the left. Enjoy yourselves.

BEATTY. Well, thank you, sir.

Clarke is there as Beatty and June leave the table.

CLARKE. Oh, Bill.

BEATTY. Hi, Nob.

CLARKE. Oh, Bill. Thank God you're here.

We note Atterley hurrying out of the Music Room and down the corridor.

Interior. Music for All: Music Room. Evening.

The Brigadier and Pugh sitting in the Visitors' Gallery. The meeting: the hall is full to overflowing. Wilson and Rubin to the side; McRae, Clarke, Castle, Carter, Richardson, Leslie, Trelawney, Garfield, Rosalind, Beatty, June, the Director, Trapnell. Military police at the back. Hubbub. Consultation and looking around. Garfield and Trapnell go down to the front. Garfield tries to attract the meeting's attention.

GARFIELD. Ladies and gentlemen . . . Ladies and gentlemen, could I have order, please . . .

Suddenly, unexpectedly, we hear Wilson:

WILSON. All rise!

The hubbub disappears speedily. Everyone stands as Rubin and Wilson process to their seats. The Brigadier looks at Pugh, Pugh doesn't know how to react. The Brigadier stands, followed by Pugh.

CLARKE. (*To McRae.*) What's going on?

MCRAE. (*To Clarke.*) I think that Rubin's being a right clever bastard, Nob.

WILSON. All sit!

Everyone sits.

RUBIN. I declare the session open. Dr Garfield.

GARFIELD. (*Very uncertain.*) Um – Ladies and gentlemen. Before the session – well, before the business starts – I have to announce a statement by the 17 Area Army Education Officer.

Reaction.

RUBIN. I recognise the Honourable and Gallant Member.

A grin spreads across McRae's face as Garfield withdraws and Trapnell begins.

TRAPNELL. Ladies and gentlemen –

SOMEONE. Honourable Members!

TRAPNELL. Yes. Yes, I'm sorry. Honourable Members. I have been – I have an announcement to read out, from the GOC.

Slight pause.

It obviously follows on from the recent unwelcome publicity that this gathering has received from a certain German gentleman.

He'd hoped for a titter. He doesn't get one.

One. The GOC British Troops in Egypt is anxious that Parliaments should continue, provided that the proceedings are conducted in order.

CARTER. (*Calling out.*) They already are!

TRAPNELL. Two. From now on, the word 'Parliament' is not to be used. This is necessary to prevent misunderstandings in press reports, etc. The word 'forum' will be substituted. Three. The proceedings are to be conducted under military control –

Reaction.

This is simply an insurance that no violent political propaganda and nothing subversive to discipline occurs. Our army as much as any other army needs to have a fine discipline if it is to win the war. Short of this there is no intention whatever to restrict the free expression of points of view.

Grumble.

Four. Proceedings will be conducted on similar lines to the Oxford Union –

Reaction:

VOICES. (*Variously.*) Oxford what? The Union? What, Transport and General?

TRAPNELL. – alternately by the 17 Area Education Officer and the RAF Education Officer. Five. The provisions of King's Regulations 541 must be observed. Six. No civilians allowed to be present.

Reaction from those not already aware of this.

This is not intended as a restrictive measure, but simply to allow maximum freedom of discussion. It is our custom to discuss social and political questions freely among ourselves: and 'hard-hitting', verbally or in the press, although well understood by us, is not . . . understood by foreigners. Seven. The GOC considers that Music for All or any similar institution is not a suitable place for holding these meetings –

Reaction!

– because of the practical difficulty of excluding strangers, and he has directed that some other place, on W.D. property, is to be found by 17 Area where the above instructions can be properly adhered to. Eight, and finally . . . The GOC points out that the War Office has already enquired about the Music for All Parliament and stated that unless these proceedings are conducted in a proper manner and according to the above instructions, he will receive orders to close down all such activities.

Pause.

That is – it.

A few reactions. A boo here, a slow handclap there. It peters out.

RUBIN. I would like to thank the Honourable and Gallant Member for his contribution . . .

Reaction. He rides it.

On which I shall rule after prayers. Please, Major.

The Padre comes to the front.

TRAPNELL. Rule?

AUDIENCE. (*Variously.*) Prayers? What's he on about, we never have prayers. What does he think this is?

MCRAE. Oh glory be. The clever effing bastard.

PADRE. Could you please, um, stand again.

As the Padre opens his prayer book, the Brigadier looks daggers at Pugh. Pugh looks most uncomfortable. The Brigadier stands. Pugh stands. Most of the rest of the audience stand too. McRae, Carter and Wilson gesture the resolutes to their feet.

PADRE. Most precious God, we humbly beseech thee, as for this kingdom in general, so especially for the High Court of parliament, under our most religious and gracious King at this time assembled . . .

Once the prayer is established, Atterley enters from outside and goes to Clarke. Atterley has a piece of paper on which he's scribbled a note. This during the next section of the prayer:

ATTERLEY. Psst. Nobby.

CLARKE. Ar?

ATTERLEY. (*Handing over the paper.*) A quote from the Military Manual. Try and get it in.

CLARKE. OK.

ATTERLEY. And, best of luck.

Meanwhile.

PADRE. That thou wouldst be pleased to direct and prosper all their consultations to the advancement of thy glory, the good of thy church, the safety, honour and welfare of our Sovereign and his Dominions; that peace and happiness, truth and justice, religion and piety, may be established among us for all generations. (*Deciding to call it a day.*) In the name of the Father, the Son and the Holy Ghost, for ever and ever. Amen.

SOME AUDIENCE. Amen.

The Padre withdraws. Everyone sits.

RUBIN. It is now my duty to rule on the matters raised by the Honourable and Gallant Member at the beginning of this session. My ruling is that these stipulations should of course be adhered to –

Protests.

– but that they clearly do not and cannot apply to these proceedings, which had of course commenced already.

Applause. The Brigadier looks black. Rubin gives a big nod to McRae.

I therefore move –

MCRAE. I spy strangers!

It takes a moment for the majority to clock that this refers to the Brigadier and Pugh. Applause.

RUBIN. I recognise the Honourable Member for Lanark, and understand his point.

He opens his 'Parliamentary procedure' at a clearly pre-marked point.

As no less a figure than the late Sir Thomas Erskine May reminds us, 'the House of Commons has always claimed and enjoyed the right to exclude strangers and to debate within closed doors. The first reason was the inconvenience caused in former times by strangers pressing into the body of the House or attempting from the galleries to influence debate. The other, and principal, reason was the possible intimidation that the crown – '

Majors wear crowns. The audience is beginning to pick up on the analogies which Rubin is obviously drawing.

' – might exercise if reports were made of the speech and actions of members, in days when freedom of debate did not in practice afford complete protection.'

He looks impishly round the room.

'According to ancient usage, the exclusion of strangers from the galleries could, at any time, be enforced without an order of the House; for, on a member taking notice of their presence, the Speaker was obliged to order them to withdraw.'

Shouts of 'withdraw' as Rubin closes the book.

Sadly, I feel that on this occasion such an order is beyond my competence.

Cries of 'oh', 'shame', 'go on'. We see Pugh and the Brigadier.

BRIGADIER. (*To Pugh.*) Is this one of ours?

PUGH. No, sir. South African.

BRIGADIER. I see.

RUBIN. I therefore call on the Prime Minister.

Clarke stands. The Brigadier looks firmly at Pugh.

CLARKE. Mr Speaker, I must say first of all that naturally we respect that there must be regulations covering the proceedings of this meeting. But I must, as – Prime Minister, I must protest most strongly at the way that this was done.

Applause.

It's surely clear what the purpose of these 'regulations' is. It is to turn this

Parliament into just a talking-shop, under military control. I can't comment on one regulation, having never been to Oxford –

Laughter and applause.

But I do know a bit about the place where I received my further education, which was here, as a member of the RAF, and I know enough to know the regulations cited in the Major's statement are quite inapplicable. (*Clarke reads Atterley's note.*) In fact, I'd ask you to listen to this quote, from the Military Manual, about what a military order is. A lawful military command 'must be', I'm quoting now, 'must be one relating to military duty, that is to say, the disobedience of it must tend to delay or impede a military proceeding'. Is it possible to ask the Major what military proceeding we're delaying or impeding? (*Applause.*) I would have thought, in fact, what we're about is helping and sustaining that great military proceeding we are all involved with, which is winning back the world for democracy and freedom. (*Applause. Clarke has an underlined passage from a pamphlet.*) When I first joined this parliament, I was – well, conscripted, into being Minister of Labour. And I was very taken with a line from Sir William Beveridge's report on social insurance. He said that 'freedom from want cannot be forced on a democracy or given to a democracy. It must be won by them.' Well, I agree with that. (*Applause.*) And so, as I've been – press-ganged into this tonight, I move a motion that: 'We object to the banning of this Parliament.'

He sits. Applause. As he's congratulated, Wilson notes down the motion.

RUBIN. The Leader of Common Wealth.

Richardson rises.

RICHARDSON. Mr Speaker, I would like to add very little to that said by the new Prime Minister. Surely, the point is that we are *not* like the German Army, we can discuss things openly, and if anything it's good for us that Goebbels or whoever has told the German people what life is like in a real citizens' army. (*Applause.*) Indeed, if we're concerned with propaganda, I think that quite unintentionally the GOC has given the German propaganda machine a much more potent weapon. The Common Wealth Party unconditionally supports the motion.

Applause as he sits.

RUBIN. The Leader of the Liberal Party.

Trelawney rises.

TRELAWNEY. Mr Speaker. Honourable Members will be aware that it is totally foreign to my nature to disagree with a word uttered either by His Majesty's Government or by His Most Loyal Opposition . . .

McRae: 'I see' look.

But I must confess that frankly I don't give a brass farthing about German propaganda.

Applause.

It seems amazing that we should even be considering re-ordering our affairs at the beck and call of Adolf Hitler.

Applause.

And the only proposal I would make would be that the proceedings of the Parliament, with suitable introductory remarks by the GOC himself, be broadcast back to Germany.

Applause.

I do not, in fact, consider that these regulations will be necessarily too onerous, but the circumstances leave me no choice, as a Liberal, but to support the motion. Thank you, Mr Speaker.

Applause. He sits.

RUBIN. The Leader of the Conservative Party.

Leslie stands. Expectant atmosphere.

LESLIE. I'm afraid that in this situation I'm in a bit of difficulty.

Laughter.

On account of not having the details of these proposals till they were read out here just now.

MCRAE. Neither did we!

LESLIE. No. No, I didn't say you did. However, I think there are three points to raise. (*Leslie continues, pedestrianly, his speech gradually reducing in volume as he goes on.*) The first is, as has been said, the Parliament decided to use party labels only as a matter of making things more realistic. As I think has been made clear. The second point is that, as the last speaker pointed out, it does seem odd, that we're instructed how to run our business by Berlin.

He looks up, perhaps expecting a smatter of applause, which doesn't happen.

The third is, that . . . (*Pause. Too long. Embarrassment. Very quietly:*) As has been also said already –

People call for Leslie to speak up.

As has been – look. (*He's off notes.*) Look. I must say this. I really must say this. This was a good thing. This was what it was supposed to be about.

Slight pause.

I mean, the Germans say, that Britain's a plutocracy. Well, do we want to prove it for them? (*He breathes deeply.*) Do we want our army to be run by – diktat? Do we want our side to be as much of a dictatorship as theirs is?

People shout No.

Well, no, of course.

He looks at his notes, trying to find a place to return to them, but he can't.

I came to this because I genuinely believed . . . I really did . . .

Pause.

I'm sorry.

He sits. Pause. Applause. Through it:

ATTERLEY. My God.

CASTLE. Does he want to get himself court-martialled?

RICHARDSON. Phew.

Applause dies.

RUBIN. I think it would be best not to take any further speeches on this subject –

Cries of 'Shame', 'Why not?', from the audience.

– in order that we may quickly proceed on to the proper business of the meeting. I shall therefore take a vote on the motion, which is –

WILSON. 'We object to the banning of the Music for All Parliament.'

RUBIN. All those in favour?

Every hand shoots up, except those of the Brigadier, Pugh, Trapnell and the Padre.

Any against?

Pause. Many people look towards the back. Slowly, the Brigadier raises his hand. The other officers look away. Amazed reaction.

There is one vote against. I declare the motion overwhelmingly carried.

Wild applause.

I now call upon the Chancellor of the Exchequer.

McRae stands. He begins his speech.

MCRAE. Mr Speaker, when I prepared my notes for this speech, I began with the words, 'this is a momentous occasion'. Well, it certainly is.

Applause. The Brigadier's eyes narrow.

We are proposing tonight to storm the central citadel of the property-owning classes.

The Brigadier rises. Pugh follows. The Brigadier leaves, followed by Colonel Pugh.

Interior. Music for All: lobby. Evening.

The Brigadier and Pugh emerge from the meeting.

BRIGADIER. I want the men who organised that demonstration.

PUGH. Um, you don't think, on the whole . . .

Interior. Music for All: Music Room. Evening.

McRae is continuing his speech:

MCRAE. The House, in brief, is being asked to pass an Act that intends to place the Banks, and thus the existing money credit system of Britain, under the control and ownership of the people.

Interior. Music for All: Music Room. Evening.

Later. Rubin is announcing the result of the Bank Nationalisation vote:

RUBIN. I now have the result of the vote on the motion that the Bill be read a second time. For, 470. Against, 52.

Applause.

I declare the motion carried. The House is – the House now stands adjourned.

Applause – heavy and prolonged. As the meeting begins to break up, Castle approaches Trapnell, as the latter makes to leave.

CASTLE. Excuse me, sir.

TRAPNELL. Yes, Castle?

CASTLE. Sir, I would suggest, that it would be useful, if the committee knew if your statement were open to negotiation.

Trapnell isn't quite sure what to say.

TRAPNELL. Well, I'm not sure if it is.

Pause.

But I suppose . . . I'll speak to them, of course.

CASTLE. Thank you, I'll tell them, sir.

The Socialists are caucusing, Clarke near them. Beatty and June approach.

BEATTY. Nob, I think, perhaps . . . that I owe you a beer.

CLARKE. I think you bloody do.

Clarke looks at his comrades, then at his mate. As this happens, Castle approaches the Socialist group.

Let's get out of here.

Clarke, Beatty and June leave.

CASTLE. Excuse me, comrades.

Wilson, McRae and Atterley look to him.

I thought I should inform you, that Major Trapnell is prepared to enter into talks about the future of the Parliament. As you know, I work with him, and I'd be happy to liaise in any way that might seem useful.

Pause.

WILSON. Thank you, uh – Graham.

CASTLE. Not at all.

He turns and goes quickly.

Interior. Bar. Night.

Crowded, noisy. June, Clarke and Beatty are sitting drinking. Their glasses are empty.

CLARKE. So I asked him, what had happened to the Agitators then, and he rushed off, and I was left there, holding, as you might –

BEATTY. – the baby –

CLARKE. I was going to say the destinies of nations . . .

BEATTY. Well, that too, right enough –

CLARKE. When in comes –

JUNE. Agitators.

CLARKE. Yuh, I said, the Cromwell –

JUNE. Yuh, I know. I know all that. I did it for matric.

CLARKE. You did?

JUNE. Uh-huh.

BEATTY. Not just a pretty face, mate. Same?

Clarke nods as Beatty stands. He picks up the glasses and we follow him to the bar, before returning to Clarke and June:

JUNE. No, what happened was, that after the debates, the debates and stuff at Putney, Cromwell got a resolution passed, to send the Agitators back, bit like demobbing I suppose. And the upshot of it was, the soldiers wouldn't swallow it, and they held this meeting where they passed this motion, well this manifesto, really, which they marched around with in their hats – you know, like trying to inspire a mutiny.

CLARKE. A mutiny.

JUNE. That's right.

CLARKE. What happened then?

JUNE. Well, as I remember, Cromwell stopped it being read out, and he packed the other regiments back off home, and three of the mutineers were sentenced to be hung. Or shot. I think it was three, anyway.

Clarke gulps his beer.

CLARKE. Oh. Right.

JUNE. But only one was. On a throw of dice. And that was more or less the end of the glorious English Revolution.

Interior. Brigadier's office. Day.

The Brigadier, Pugh, Signals Colonel, the Other Colonel, and others.

BRIGADIER. It seems both mutinies lasted longer than their chaps expected. The conclusion of the Alex mutiny was the boarding of the ships by local Greek forces, the disarming of the mutineers, and their arrest. Casualties in the operation were thirty. The Burg-el-Arab thing was in fact ended by Allied forces, who outnumbered the four thousand or so Greeks blockaded in the desert camp. There were no Greek deaths, but one British officer was killed in the operation.

OTHER COLONEL. When you say 'Allied Forces'?

BRIGADIER. They were mainly Indians.

OTHER COLONEL. And was the decision to employ wog troops in any way connected with fears that if actual British troops were used, they might refuse the job?

Pause.

BRIGADIER. Well, we know the score. Leaflets were issued, emanating from civilian bolshies here in Cairo, in liaison, we believe, with some elements of the stationed British troops. There is also evidence that food supplies were smuggled into Burg-el-Arab and of course we can't be sure no British ORs were involved.

OTHER COLONEL. Didn't the gyppo police come up with something –

BRIGADIER. Yes, there was evidence of some collusion.

Pause.

Are there any other questions?

Pause.

Well, in that case, let us move on to item five.

OTHER COLONEL. The connected item five.

BRIGADIER. Um – Raymond.

PUGH. Well, the matter really is contained in the report before you.

Interior. Music for All: committee. Day.

A meeting of the Parliamentary Committee, attended by Trapnell, Garfield, McRae, Wilson, Atterley, Castle, Richardson, Carter, Trelawney and Leslie. Everyone has a copy of Trapnell's order. During this sequence, Wilson is busy taking notes.

TRAPNELL. Gentlemen, I have very little to add, beyond saying that your committee will of course continue to administer the new forum, though under the chairmanship of the Area Education Officer. (*With a smile.*) Which is me. (*Slight pause.*) The other point is that the venue of the forum will be the Kasr el Nil Barracks gymnasium.

A low-level reaction: intakes of breath, looks.

I would be happy to answer any questions.

WILSON. I'd like to ask the Major who was responsible for this announcement?

TRAPNELL. It came to the Education Officer from the Area Commander Brigadier, on the order of Commander BTE.

MCRAE. Is this the only Parliament to be stopped?

TRAPNELL. I'm afraid I don't know.

CARTER. So this 'order' doesn't cover other Parliaments? Like in the RAF?

TRAPNELL. No, not as far –

CARTER. So does that mean that if we substituted RAF men for the army members on the Parliament committee, we could carry on?

Some chuckles.

TRAPNELL. No, I don't think that I would advise that, I'm afraid.

Pause.

WILSON. On the question of civilians, you do know that civilians can be excluded from certain Music for All functions?

TRAPNELL. I really don't think the question of the new location is negotiable.

ATTERLEY. Can we know what is the position of the Speaker of the Parliament?

TRAPNELL. I think the Chairman of the Forum will be someone else.

RICHARDSON. Can you say who else?

TRAPNELL. (*With a slight smile.*) I suspect it will be me.

LESLIE. Look, Major. You have made it clear this 'announcement' is an order. Does this mean we're ordered to take part in this thing in the gymnasium?

TRAPNELL. No, I think – no.

Slight pause.

It is impossible to order someone to take part in a voluntary activity.

Slight pause. He looks round. Pause.

Look, um. I didn't know.

Slight pause.

I must assure you, gentlemen, until the day before, I didn't know.

He stands.

Now, unless there's any further . . .

No one says anything.

Right. Good afternoon.

He goes quickly, almost bumping into Beatty in the corridor.

WILSON. Now, may I suggest, a reply on these rough lines . . .

Amusement that Wilson has got something drafted already.

One. The Committee . . .

BEATTY. 'Scuse me.

They look at him.

Is this the Parliament committee?

GARFIELD. Yes, that's correct.

BEATTY. I'm Beatty. Heliopolis. I'm a mate of Nobby Clarke. And I thought you'd want to know, he's just been picked up by a couple of MPs, for posting.

MCRAE. What?

LESLIE. Oh, no.

Slight pause.

WILSON. Alf Jacobs. Simp.

Pause.

ATTERLEY. I'd say – you need to get this out. I'd say, you need news of this to get to London.

CARTER. We.

ATTERLEY. Beg your pardon?

CARTER. *We* need news of this to get to London.

Exterior. Desert. Day.

Clarke is in a truck sitting beside an MP. Another MP is driving. A moment or two, then:

CLARKE. Is it just me?

> *The MP raises an eyebrow but says nothing.*

D'you know? Is it just me?

> *Pause.*

I mean, there were four hundred people there. There must have been, what, twenty speakers? Presumably I'm not the only person who you're picking up.

> *Pause.*

Are you ordered not to speak to me?

Interior. GHQ Public Relations: corridor. Day.

McRae jaunts along the corridor, whistling the Marseillaise. Ballantine sticks his head out of the cuttings room. He enters his office.

BALLANTINE. Well, you sound bright enough this morning.

MCRAE. Well, it's being so . . .

Interior. GHQ Public Relations: office. Day.

McRae enters the office. We – and he – see Carrington at his desk first.

MCRAE. So sorry, sir. Tied up at –

CARRINGTON. Alistair.

McRae sees the MP standing by his desk.

I'm sorry.

Interior. AEC Office. Day.

We start on a typewriter:

Already typed: To Hugh Lawson MP House of Commons In addition to the info in my last gram to Pritt should add one participant already

Now being typed: posted destination unknown

A pen comes into shot and inserts 'at least' before 'one participant'. We see the typist is Graham Castle.

Interior. Embarkation Unit: office. Day.

The officer-in-charge – a Captain – is sitting at his desk. He looks up. McRae is there with two Army sergeants. We may recognise the Second Sergeant.

OFFICER-IN-CHARGE. McRae.

MCRAE. Yes, sir. Am I under arrest?

OFFICER-IN-CHARGE. This is an embarkation unit, McRae. It deals with transport in and out of Egypt.

MCRAE. Yes, I'm aware of that, sir. Am I under arrest?

OFFICER-IN-CHARGE. Well, in a sense –

MCRAE. So when will I be charged then, sir?

Pause.

Do you propose to keep me under lock and key?

OFFICER-IN-CHARGE. All right. Just hold your horses, McRae.

He nods at the Sergeants, who take McRae out. The officer-in-charge picks up the phone.

Interior. Embarkation Unit: barracks. Day.

The dormitory is empty. McRae is brought in by the two Sergeants.

MCRAE. So. Do you know where they're sending me?

SECOND SERGEANT. Heard, the Persian Gulf.

FIRST SERGEANT. The White Man's grave.

MCRAE. I see.

> *The first Sergeant goes out. The Second makes to follow but turns back. We note that he has a strong Lancastrian accent.*

SECOND SERGEANT. Eh. Jock.

MCRAE. Yes, what?

SECOND SERGEANT. A message. Marathon.

MCRAE. You what?

SECOND SERGEANT. I'd guess – the news got through.

> *He winks and goes. Head back round again.*

Oh, and the Reds are in Odessa.

Interior. Music for All: Pergola Cafeteria. Day.

Wilson, Atterley, Carter and Castle sitting with drinks. Wilson is reading a British newspaper cutting – a Parliamentary Report:

WILSON. 'Mr Pritt asked if the secretary of state was aware that at the meeting of the "Forces Parliament", held on etcetera etcetera . . . whether he would immediately reverse this treatment and, in particular, direct that the threats to post the leaders of the protest be not carried out.'

> *Wilson looks up.*

CARTER. Go on, for heaven's sake.

WILSON. Sir James Grigg, Secretary of State for War. 'I am expecting a report on this. If the Commander-in-Chief has intervened – '

GARFIELD. (*Out of vision.*) Uh, gentlemen.

They look up to see Garfield. He holds a piece of paper. He's furious.

GARFIELD. I'm sorry to disturb you. But there are two things that you ought to know. The first is that the Commander of 17 Area, British Troops in Egypt, has issued a report which blames me, *me*, for the 'demonstration' of the 5th of April. For not 'bringing influence to bear'.

Slight pause.

The second is that I have discovered that my first telegram to D. N. Pritt was stopped. A telegram, from an American civilian, to a British Parliamentary representative. And I must tell you, I am prepared to lodge a protest, with my consulate, in the strongest possible . . .

Slight pause.

In the strongest possible terms.

He turns and goes.

WILSON. So, how on earth . . .

They sense that Castle may have the answer. They turn to him.

CASTLE. Never you mind.

Interior. Embarkation Unit: corridor. Day.

McRae waits sitting on the bench outside the Officer-in-Charge's office. The two Sergeants are either side of him. The Officer-in-Charge comes out of his office. McRae stands.

FIRST SERGEANT. Tenshun.

McRae to attention.

OFFICER-IN-CHARGE. Sergeant McRae. You are being posted.

MCRAE. Posted? When, sir?

OFFICER-IN-CHARGE. Now.

MCRAE. The Persian Gulf?

Slight pause.

OFFICER-IN-CHARGE. No. What have the Persians ever done to us? To Liverpool.

McRae can't believe it.

MCRAE. But, sir, I signed for the duration –

OFFICER-IN-CHARGE. Did you now.

Slight pause.

You're going back to Blighty, McRae. And it's welcome to you. Sergeant!

He goes back into his office.

FIRST SERGEANT. Jammy sod.

SECOND SERGEANT. Give my regards to Macclesfield.

McRae remembers the Second Sergeant as the Lancastrian in the King's Speech meeting.

Interior. Gymnasium. Evening.

A huge room. Chairs set out in long, neat rows. At the front, a table, at which Trapnell and Pugh sit. Castle sits in the front row. A War Correspondent stands to the side. Long pause. Then a couple comes in. An RAF Corporal and a WAAF. They stand there.

PUGH. Good evening. Welcome to the Forces Forum.

CORPORAL. Um . . .

Pause. The Corporal and the WAAF whisper. Then the Corporal, to Pugh:

CORPORAL. I'm sorry, sir. We were actually looking round for somewhere quiet.

Pause. They turn and quickly go.

TRAPNELL. Well, you found it.

Pause.

PUGH. You know what worries me, John?

TRAPNELL. What's that, sir?

PUGH. It's not so much that they could get six hundred people to turn up, but that they can then get them all to stay away.

Pause. Trapnell lights his pipe. Pause. Castle can't repress what comes out like a cough but is clearly a snigger.

TRAPNELL. Shut up, Castle.

Interior. Brigadier's Office. Day.

Wilson standing in front of the Brigadier's desk, on which is lying a letter.

BRIGADIER. Now, Warrant Officer, I gather that you've got a problem.

WILSON. Well, sir, it's more of a complaint.

BRIGADIER. Complaint?

WILSON. That my mail is being interfered with.

BRIGADIER. Now, I wonder, do you mean this letter?

WILSON. Yes, sir.

BRIGADIER. Well, I stopped it.

WILSON. Yes.

Pause.

Sir, I had understood from both my Colonel and the Chief Military Censor that my letter had been passed, and actually posted, sir.

BRIGADIER. I'm sorry, Warrant Officer, but you can't have heard me properly. I said *I* stopped it.

WILSON. On what ground, sir?

Pause. The Brigadier leans back in his chair.

BRIGADIER. You know, Warrant Officer . . . I'm a Book man. Always been my motto. Read the Book, and then do what it tells you. (*He taps a shirt pocket, in which we see the bulge of a small book.*) King's Regulations. Like a Bible. Always with me. (*He smiles benignly.*) If you want to make this thing official, then of course you're utterly within your rights. Good day, then, Warrant Officer.

Interior. Outer Office. Day.

Wilson comes out of the Brigadier's office. He stands for a moment. In the outer office, a Corporal is typing. He was at the last Parliament. Wilson nods at him, the Corporal hardly responds, Wilson makes to go.

GHQ CORPORAL. (*Not looking up from his work.*) Uh – sir.

WILSON. Yes, Corporal?

With the slightest of surreptitious looks around him, the Corporal removes the page he is typing and hands it to Wilson.

GHQ CORPORAL. Might be of interest, sir. The door is there.

Wilson takes the piece of paper, pockets it and moves.

Interior. Music for All: Pergola Cafeteria. Day.

Wilson and Atterley sitting over beers in the Pergola garden of Music for All.

WILSON. (*Reads.*) 'W.O. Cable. Yesterday a.m.: No further postings in connection Cairo Forces Parliament.' And 'on 6.4.44 postings list, 1, Sgt A. McRae, 2, AC2 G. Clarke, WO S. Wilson, 12'.

He looks to Atterley.

ATTERLEY. I am so sorry, Steve.

WILSON. You bugger off.

He finds a lighter, sets fire to paper in an ashtray. We hear Castle's voice:

CASTLE. (*Out of vision.*) Comrades.

They look up and see him.

WILSON. Hello, Graham. Sit you down.

CASTLE. Yes, thanks.

He sits.

ATTERLEY. Hey, is something up?

CASTLE. Well, you could say that. I've been discharged.

WILSON. *You've* been discharged?

CASTLE. Over the telegrams to Pritt and Lawson. And being generally, 'temperamentally unfit'. As a holder of the King's commission.

Pause.

ATTERLEY. Well, bugger that.

CASTLE. Indeed.

Pause. Wilson is trying to attract a waiter's eye.

WILSON. Look, let's get you sorted with a drink.

CASTLE. Well, actually no.

Slight pause. He stands.

No, I ought to . . . quite a lot of things.

ATTERLEY. Yes. Yes, of course.

They smile, not quite sure what to say.

CASTLE. You know, I heard, they're putting all the railings back up. You know, that they took down from the private parks in London. They're going back up, so I hear.

Pause.

Well, then. Goodbye.

WILSON. Goodbye.

ATTERLEY. Good luck.

He turns and goes. Pause. Wilson and Atterley sip their beer.

WILSON. You know, Nobby Clarke came up to me, just before the April meeting, and asked me what happened after the New Model Army had written the Agreement of the People. I didn't have the heart to tell him.

ATTERLEY. No?

Pause.

You know, you really ought to trust the masses, Steve.

WILSON. I'm sorry?

ATTERLEY. Well, it didn't end. With the executions. It went on. Small mutinies, rebellions, demonstrations, flaring up, without warning or advertisement, all over England.

WILSON. Good.

Pause.

My father once saw Churchill. He was standing in a barge, that's Churchill, not my pa, in the middle of the Rhine, in 1919, trying to calm the troops who hadn't been demobbed and who were being threatened with the Eastern Front. And it had to be a barge, 'cos otherwise they would have chucked him in.

He drains his beer.

Well, time to get back. I've at least three files to sort this afternoon.

He looks at Atterley.

No, I think you're right. They won't allow the railings to go up again.

He makes to go. He turns back, as if he wants to ask Atterley's opinion. But then he changes his mind, and goes. Neville Atterley smiles and sips his beer.

Exterior. English countryside. Day.

A train, puffing its way through the English countryside.

Interior. Train. Day.

Inside the train. Servicemen and women. Some wounded. After a moment or two, we see Nobby Clarke.

Exterior. Station. Day.

The train pulls into a station. Waiting people, mostly women. A few servicemen, including some wounded, get out of the train. Wives and girlfriends rush to greet and embrace them. A paper boy on the platform:

PAPERBOY. Mirr-er. Daily Mirr-er.

Interior. Train. Day.

The train is still stationary. Clarke hears the boy and looks out.

CLARKE. A paper, please.

PAPERBOY. (*Handing one over.*) That's one penny, sir.

CLARKE. (*Paying.*) Thank you.

Clarke looks at the cover.

It's the famous 5 July 1945 cover of the Daily Mirror: the Zec cartoon of a wounded, bandaged, battered private soldier, handing back a laurel wreath labelled 'Victory and Peace in Europe', with the caption: 'Here you are – don't lose it again'. Above is the headline: 'Don't lose it again'. Beside is the headline of the front-page leader: 'Vote for Them'.

Clarke takes it in, then quickly calls to the paperboy again:

Hey, boy! boy!

PAPERBOY. (*Returning.*) Yes, sir?

CLARKE. I'll take the lot. However many you've got there.

PAPERBOY. But, I've got more than thirty, sir.

A whistle blows.

CLARKE. Come *on.*

The other servicemen look on at crazy Clarke, as the paperboy counts the papers. After a few moments, Clarke, impatiently:

So, how much?

PAPERBOY. That's two and ninepence, sir.

Whistle again.

CLARKE. Two and – Three bob. Keep the change.

Clarke just manages to pay the boy before the train starts to move. Clarke tears off the front page of a copy of the paper. To the other servicemen and women:

In the windows. All along the train.

Exterior. Another station. Day.

Relatives, wives, waiting at another station. Then we see the train. The 'Vote for Them' front page has been stuck up in all the windows, all along the train. The wives and relatives waiting on the platform watch as the train draws into the station: the frame freezing on the poster itself before the train comes to a halt. We hear the voice of the present-day Nobby Clarke.

CLARKE. (*Voice over.*) Now as everybody knows, it was the troops who won Labour the election in 1945. And in that sense brought about the NHS, the welfare state, the things we argued for. And in retrospect it makes me proud, to have played a part in that, but it also makes me angry.

Interior. Room. Day.

Close-up of the present-day Clarke being interviewed.

CLARKE. Because the things we won are being ripped apart. Because personally we've reached an age we might find we've got a use for them ourselves. But most of all because everything that's happening now, it seems to me, sets back the chance of anything like what we did happening again.

Slight pause.

And that angers me because they told us at the time we couldn't do it and it wouldn't work. And we did it and it did work. And I think that ought to be remembered.

Run caption:

The characters in this play are invented. However, it is based on real events, and the memories of those who participated in them:

Leo Abse, John Banks, Sam Bardell, Don Brayford, Norman Bucknall, Bill Davidson, Basil Davidson, Basil Goldstone, Alec Grant, Mark Hinson, Mike Katanka, Hugh Lawson, Albert Levine, Pete Perry, Bob Snodgrass, Syd Stott, W. J. (Buck) Taylor, Johnny Walker, Dave Wallis.

Closing titles of Episode Three.